COLLECTED POEMS

Moya Cannon is an Irish poet with six published
collections, the most recent being *Donegal Tarantella*
(Carcanet). The mountains, the shoreline and our
primal and enduring responses to the beauty of the
endangered earth are the inspiration for many of
her poems. Archaeology and geology figure too as
gateways to deeper understanding of our mysterious
relationship with the natural world and our past.
    Music, particularly traditional Irish music, has
always been a deep interest and is a constant theme.
She has received the Brendan Behan Award and the
O'Shaughnessy Award and was 2011 Heimbold Pro-
fessor of Irish Studies at Villanova University. She
was born in Co. Donegal and now lives in Dublin.

Moya Cannon

COLLECTED POEMS

CARCANET

First published in Great Britain in 2021 by
Carcanet
Alliance House, 30 Cross Street
Manchester M2 7AQ
www.carcanet.co.uk

A CIP catalogue record for this book is
available from the British Library.

ISBN 978 1 80017 032 2

Book design by Andrew Latimer
Printed in Great Britain by SRP Ltd, Exeter, Devon

The publisher acknowledges financial
assistance from Arts Council England.

CONTENTS

11. *The Parchment Boat* (1997)

III. *Carrying the Songs* (2007)

IV. *Hands* (2011)

v. *Keats Lives* (2015)

VII. *New Poems*

PREFACE

I agree with Wisława Szymborska when she says, 'Whatever inspiration is, it is born from a continuous "I don't know"'. We sit down to write poems as teenagers or young adults to try to sort out our confused feelings and ideas about something which has shaken us or affected us profoundly. Half a lifetime later, some of us look up to find ourselves still at the same task. A poem can entertain contradiction in the same way that our lives often entertain contradictions. Perhaps this is why, as readers and also as writers, we turn to poetry in our darkest and in our brightest hours, in desperation and in rapture. Poems, like music, can chart the territories at the edges of our psychic maps, the 'Here be Dragons' and the 'Hy-Brasils'. Sometimes they are the only charts available to us.

I regard myself as having been extraordinarily fortunate in the culture I encountered as a child, where poetry was regarded as important. As a young adult in the 1970s, rapid and exciting changes were occurring within that culture. I came of age and started to write during a great age of translation, when English language poetry was being increasingly influenced and refreshed by Asian, Eastern European, Spanish and South American poetry and also by the cultural revolution of the 1960s. This was also the time when women's voices became central to poetry and poetic discourse. Movements of population and culture in the twenty-first century, particularly from Asia and Africa, are again renewing and re-energising English-language poetry.

Collected Poems includes almost all the poems from my six collections: *Oar* (1990), *The Parchment Boat* (1997), *Carrying the Songs* (1907), *Hands* (2011), *Keats Lives* (2015) and *Donegal Tarantella* (2019). I have made minor changes to a few poems. My first collection, *Oar*, was edited by Jessie Lendennie and Mike Allen of Salmon Publishing, Galway, who took great care with the production and proofreading, with the quality of the paper and with the printing of the cover illustration. This collection was republished in 1994, when Salmon came under the wing of Poolbeg Press. *The Parchment Boat* was carefully edited and published by Peter and Jean Fallon of Gallery Press, who also republished *Oar* in 2000. The subsequent four collections were meticulously edited by Judith Willson, Luke Allan, Andrew Latimer and Michael Schmidt of Carcanet Press. I take this opportunity to thank all of the above editors for their attentive and painstaking work.

I warmly thank the Tyrone Guthrie Centre; The Pier Arts Centre, Orkney; Trent University, Ontario; Kerry Co. Council; Waterford Co. Council; The Verbal Arts Centre, Derry; *Le Centre Culturel Irlandais,* Paris; The Virginia Centre for the Creative Arts; the *Centre d'Art i Natura de Farrera, Catalunya,* and The Heinrich Böll Cottage, Achill, for their gracious hospitality during the writing of some of these poems. Sincere thanks are also due to Charles A. Heimbold and the Department of Irish Studies at Villanova University for a fruitful semester spent there. Gratitude is due to Aosdána and the Arts Council of Ireland which have made it possible for me, and for many others, to pursue writing as a profession. Special thanks are due also to my friends, Kathleen Loughnane, Mary Armstrong and Michael Coady, and to my husband, John Roden, who have often been the first readers of my poems. Finally, I would also like to thank John for his unfailing patience and support on so many fronts and for his wizardry with matters technological.

for John

I
OAR

(1990)

EAGLES' ROCK

Predators and carrion crows still nest here,
falcons, and this pair of ravens
that I first heard when I reached the cairn
and noticed a narrow skull among the stones.

Here, further east at the cliff,
their wing-tips touch the rock below me,
and leave,
and touch again.

Black as silk, they know their strong corner of the sky.
They circle once
and once
and once
and once again and soar out
to sweep their territory of bright grey hills.

There are green slashes down there,
full of wells and cattle,
and higher places, where limestone, fertile,
catacombed, breaks into streams and gentians.

Predators have nested here in late winter,
have swung against this face —
feather arrogant against stone —
long enough to name it.

Once Colman, the dove saint,
lived under this cliff,
left us his oratory, his well,
and his servant's grave.

The eagles are hunted, dead,
but down among the scrub and under the hazels
this summer's prey tumbles already
out of perfect eggs.

HOLY WELL

Water returns, hard and bright,
out of the faulted hills.

Rain that flowed
down through the limestone's pores
until dark streams hit bedrock
now finds a way back,
past the roots of the ash,
to a hillside pen
of stones and statues.

Images of old fertilities
testify to nothing more, perhaps,
than the necessary miracle
of water trapped and stored
in a valley where water is fugitive.

A chipped and tilted Mary
grows green among rags and sticks.
Her trade dwindles —
bad chests, rheumatic pains,
the supplications, mostly, and the confidences of old age.

Yet sometimes,
swimming out in waters
that were blessed in the hill's labyrinthine heart,
the eel flashes past.

THIRST IN THE BURREN

No ground or floor
is as kind to the human step
as the rain-cut flags
of these white hills.

Porous as skin,
limestone resounds sea-deep, time-deep,
yet, in places, rainwater has worn it thin
as a fish's fin.

From funnels and clefts
ferns arch their soft heads.

A headland full of water, dry as bone,
with only thirst as a diviner,
thirst of the inscrutable fern
and the human thirst
that beats upon a stone.

WEST

Between high walls
the grass grows greenest.
These limestone walls
have no need of gates.
The room-sized fields,
with their well-made gaps,
open onto one another
in a great puzzle
of fragile wall and pasture
and more gaps.

Only occasionally will we find
an animal caught
in a cropped field
without gate or gap.

OAR

Walk inland and inland
with your oar,
until someone asks you
what it is.

Then build your house.

For only then will you need to tell and know
that the sea is immense and unfathomable,
that the oar that pulls
against the wave
and with the wave
is everything.

THALASSA

Having got up, decided to go home,
how often do we find ourselves
walking in the wrong direction.

Some echo under the stones
seduces our feet,
leads them down again
by the grey, agitated sea.

'TAOM'

The unexpected tide,
the great wave,
uncontained, breasts the rock,
overwhelms the heart, in spring or winter.

Surfacing from a fading language,
the word comes when needed.
A dark sound surges and ebbs,
its accuracy steadying the heart.

Certain kernels of sound
reverberate like seasoned timber,
unmuted truths of a people's winters,
stirrings of a thousand different springs.

There are small unassailable words
that diminish Caesars;
territories of the voice
that intimate across death and generation
how a secret was imparted —
that first articulation,
when a vowel was caught
between a strong and a tender consonant,
when someone, in anguish,
made a new and mortal sound
that lived until now,
a testimony
to waves succumbed to
and survived.

TREE STUMP

Thrown up
on the stones
in a bad November,

tree stump
returned from an exile
amongst fish and cormorants.

For a week or a year
the ocean has salted your huge wound,
rocks have battered off your bark,
but the shipworms haven't riddled you.

Alive or dead,
there is little left of the slow strength
that filled a sky
when summer followed winter
and wind threw down the seeds.

I drag off bladderwrack
to look at the years
and find, hugged hard
in the wilderness of your roots,
lumps of granite
that stunted
and informed your growth.

TURF BOATS

Black hookers at anchor
shining sea cattle;
rough trees for masts
rooted in salt water;
built, not for slaughter,
but for a life-giving traffic.

Wide ribs of oak,
a human heart filled you
as you sailed out of Carna.
You came into Kilronan,
two sods went flying,
you carried fire to the islands,
lime to Connemara.

Hollow boats at the Claddagh,
hearts that beat in you
lie in granite-walled graveyards
from Leitirmullen to Barna,
finished with hardship,
the unloading of cargo,
the moody Atlantic
that entered the marrow,
and bright days off Ceann Boirne,
when wind struck the brown sails
and Ithaca was Carna.

PRODIGAL

Dark mutter tongue,
rescue me,
I am drawn into outrageous worlds
where there is no pain or innocence,
only the little quiet sorrows
and the elegant joys of power.

Someone,
businesslike in his desires,
has torn out the moon by its roots.
Oh, my tin king is down now, mother,
down and broken,
my clear-browed king
who seemed to know no hungers
has killed himself.
Old gutter mother,
I am bereft now,
my heart has learnt nothing
but the stab of its own hungers
and the murky truth of a half-obsolete language
that holds at least the resonance
of the throbbing, wandering earth.

Try to find me stones and mud now, mother,
give me somewhere to start,
green and struggling, a blade under snow,
for this place and age demand relentlessly
something I will never learn to give.

What knot at the root of articulation is loosening,
have we said too much?
The old trees are coming down to the river to drink
and the young trees on the mountain
are tormented by this, their first autumn.
Who now can plant a finger on the loss
or deny the bereavement?

We thought only to bring clarity
out of the murk of utterance,
a modicum of control,
a necessary precision
and, perhaps, an elegance.

But we find
that in this damned garden by the river
we have bred pheasants;
it hardly matters whether we feed them or shoot.

Where now is the fine drive of abstraction,
where our dim talk on pillows?
Where are our black ships at anchor?
And, above all, of what use is it to us to know
that the old dirty languages still hold
touch in the ear,
lick in the ear,
secrets for everybody?

We are no longer everybody.
Half-individuated we suffer,
unable to assuage the hungers
in the head, the heart, the blood.
Our dreams differ now,
one from the other,
so that we cannot converse on pillows
and our gods quarrel endlessly.

We, who have conquered,
weep dry tears,
unable to lament our loss —
the tongue's tangle
of comfort and fear.

We know well that
if we had sense we would know
that the river is stealing the bank,
tugging it down streams by the long grass,
while under our feet,
leaves lie that are red as dragons
and the very stones are ambiguous.

Have we said too little
too clearly,
our parsimony a theft?
Who now is there to assert
that there was love among the barbarous daffodils
when leaves were green as spears?

HILLS

My wild hills come stalking.
Did I perhaps after all, in spite of all,
try to cast them off,
my dark blue hills,
that were half the world's perimeter?
Have I stooped so low as to lyricise about heather,
adjusting my love
to fit elegantly
within the terms of disinterested discourse?

Who do I think I'm fooling?
I know these hills better than that.
I know them blue, like delicate shoulders.
I know the red grass that grows in high boglands
and the passionate brightnesses and darknesses
of high bog lakes.
And I know too how,
in the murk of winter,
these wet hills will come howling through my blood
like wolves.

THE FOOT OF MUCKISH

People from our town on the coast
cut turf at the foot of Muckish.
Other than that,
it was beyond our pale.

But one evening, coming down off Muckish
when I was ten, a clumsy, dark-hearted child,
I came over the last shoulder
and the small black mountain opposite
rose up in a cliff
and rocked a lake between its ankles.

A sixpence,
a home for all the little dark streams,
a moon
in the miles of acid land.

LISTENING CLAY
for Catriona

There are sounds
that we can,
and do, trust;

    a gale in the trees,
    the soft click of stones, where the tide falls back,
    a baby crying in the night.

No one has ever mocked these sounds,
or tried to comprehend them.
They are too common to be bought or sold,
they were here before the word,
and have no significance in law.

Endlessly repeated,
immutable,
they are sounds without a history.
They comfort and disturb
the clay part of the heart.

EASTER

We went down through gardens where the trees moved,
the gates to the swamp were thrown open
and we were lost to the sprouting earth.

We were down among the old easters
where passion unmade us into our elements.
In that warm dark, only the blind heart ploughed on
as though the terrain were known.

SCAR

Why does it affect
and comfort me,
the little scar,
where, years ago, you cut your lip
shaving when half-drunk
and in a hurry
to play drums in public.

We step now
to rhythms we don't own or understand
and, with blind, dog-like diligence,
we hunt for scars
in tender places.

EROS

To be with you, my love,
is not at all like being in heaven
but like being in the earth.

Like hazelnuts
we sleep
and dream faint memories of a life
when we were high, green, among leaves;
a life given
in a time of callow innocence,
before storms came
and we all fell down,
rattled down cold streams,
caught in the stones,
while berries, seasons, flowed past.
Then quicker currents, elvers, dislodged us,
nudged us out into the flow,
rushed us down with black leaf-debris,
and swept on
forgetting us
on some river-bend or delta.

For us, drifted together,
this is the time when shells are ready
for that gentler breaking.

The deep and tender earth
assails us with dreams,
breaks us,
nourishes us,
as we tug apart
its own black crust.

AFTERLOVE
for Colman

How could I have forgotten
the sickness,
the inescapability?
My strange love,
it frightens my life.
We sail high seas
and watch the voyages of stars.
Sometimes they collide.
Did you know, you make my head flame.
Blue flames and purple flames leap about my head.
I had once a thousand tongues
but tonight
my head is crashing through the sky,
my head is flaming on a dish.

My love,
carry it in carefully,
my love,
carry it in with trumpets.

NARROW GATHERINGS

At Portrush
the boarding houses are empty
even along the sea-front.
How quiet a Sunday
for after Easter.
Up to the tall houses
the pale tide flows
disturbed and beautiful,
the April sun barely brightens
its legendary cold.

Lir's children had it hardest here,
and here
the giants sculpted rock to honeycomb,
hammered back the great arched cliffs,
but failed to join two shores.

Encumbered by legend,
we are foreigners here
and know less
than we had imagined.

A band, practising in the town, winds
now out of wind-scraped streets,
the policeman first
and the great drums
that come and come like summer thunder

and then the flutes and fifes —
a music unexpected
as silver water collected
in the dark shoulders of hills, caught,
and gathered narrow for an instant
under high wrists,
until the wind splits it finely,
a young river scattering.

Under a low sun
the band is marching now
past the painted doors

and down along the promenade,
towards the cold shore and turning
until all the wind-snatched silver life strikes
bright against the tide:

And after
come the marching children,
growing smaller and smaller
in their uniforms.

DARK SPRING
i.m. Feilimí Ó hUallacháin

Last night
the sky was still so full of light
the birds shouted in the empty trees
when, in the bone the dark cracked,
with so little sound,
almost no sound,
we did not hear it
but, incredulous, saw in our grief
the dark birds falling out of every tree
and after the birds the falling, dead, dark leaves.
Oh, we wept, we were not told,
we were not led to expect,
back when the thin bone knit to close the sky,
inside the skull-cave when we etched our myths
and later made our compacts with the ogre
we had no thought of this,
nor could we have schooled our hearts for this absurd
and sudden
sorrow.

Fair head
so vivid, in the loose wet earth.

In your death we are twice lost, twice bereaved,
all our compacts now dissolved,
we are so unexpectedly mortal.

Yet even
as we leave you
the sun flies down
to strike the dark hills green.
Defiant, it drives the pulse of summer
through this most desolate spring.

WET DOVES

Two wet doves are perched in the tree all afternoon.

On a day as rainy as this,
a bare apple tree is a poor place to roost.

Beyond my window
this tatty metaphor of love and fructitude huddles
and grubs under its oxters
and defecates and drips
and then
spreads two perfectly white fans
and flies away.

ANNALS

Rocks were fitted
to round the tops of narrow windows.
When they got to the doorway,
the monks had chisels,
so they carved the faces of saints.

Moling and Fiachra,
blurred by twelve centuries,
gaze from their romanesque arch
into the hazels,
remembering the time the mad king
came down out of the trees at last,
ate humble pie,
and, with some misgivings,
took to a foreign religion.

Clapped to the church's other end,
a handball alley complete
with decayed timber seats
shares a fifteenth century window.
The Hibernian colosseum
stands derelict within the century,
hardly a cypher now in the annals
of the Kilkenny County Board.

But now that the tree king, and the monks
and the handball-players are dust,
the last lay recited,
the last malediction lifted,
the last protest contested,

a thrush nesting in the doorway
shifts slightly on her eggs,
and awaits the millennium.

NEST

A brown wheel of reeds and broken willow
turns somnolently in a corner above the weir.
How long will that current hold it
before the flow sweeps it over?

Two Coke cans and a fast-food carton
are wound into the heart of it.

Out of habit,
god goes on making nests.

CROW'S NEST

On St Stephen's Day,
near the cliffs on Horn Head,
I came upon a house,
the roof-beams long since rotted into grass
and, outside, a little higher than the lintels,
a crow's nest in a dwarf tree.

A step up from the bog
into the crown of the ash,
the nest is a great tangled heart;
heather sinew, long blades of grass,
wool and a feather,
wound and wrought
with all the energy and art
that's in a crow.

Did crows ever build so low before?
Were they deranged, the pair who nested here,
or the other pair who built the house behind the tree,
or is there no place too poor or wild
to support,
if not life,
then love, which is the hope of it,
for who knows whether the young birds lived?

AFTER THE BURIAL

They straightened the blankets,
piled her clothes onto the bed,
soaked them with petrol,
then emptied the gallon can
over the video and tape recorder,
stepped outside their trailer,
lit it, watched until only the burnt chassis was left,
gathered themselves
and pulled out of Galway.

Camped for a week in Shepherd's Bush,
then behind a glass building in Brixton,
he went into drunken mourning for his dead wife,
while their children hung around the vans,
or foraged in the long North London streets
among other children,
some of whom also perhaps understood
that, beyond respectability's pale,
where reason and civility show their second face,
it's hard to lay ghosts.

SYMPATHETIC VIBRATION
for Kathleen

'You never strike a note,
you always *take* the note.'

Did it take her many
of her eighty quiet passionate years
to earn that knowledge,
or was it given?

Music, the dark tender secret of it,
is locked into the wood of every tree.
Yearly it betrays its presence
in minute fistfuls of uncrumpling green.

No stroke or blade can release the music
which is salve to ease the world's wounds,
which tells and, modulating, retells
the story of our own groping roots,
of the deep sky from which they retreat
and, in retreating, reach —
the tree's great symphony of leaf.

No stroke or blade can bring us that release
but sometimes, where wildness has not been stilled,
hands, informed by years of patient love,
can come to know the hidden rhythms of the wood,
can touch bow to gut
and take the note,
as the heart yields and yields
and sings.

FOUNDATIONS

Digging foundations for a kitchen,
a foot and a half below the old concrete
they open a midden of seashells.

This was once called 'kitchen' —
poor man's meat, salty, secretive,
gathered at low spring tide.

Blue mussels creaked as a hand twisted them from the cluster,
limpets were banged off with a stone, lifted with a blade,
the clam's breathing deep in wet sand
gave a mark to the spade.

Backs ached, reaping the cold and succulent harvest.
How many were consumed?

A shovelful, two shovelfuls,
six barrowloads, are dug out and dumped —
the midden runs under the wall
into the neighbour's yard.
The builder goes home, joking that he's found gold.

In a battered barrow, under the June evening sun,
the last shovelfuls turn palest gold.
They speak in silent sympathy
with all that has been exiled, killed and hidden,
then exhumed,
vulnerable again in the air of another age.

The taciturn clams break their silence to say,
'Dig us out if you need to,
position the steel,
raise the concrete walls,
but, when your shell is complete,
remember that your life,
no less than ours,
is measured by the tides of the sea
and is unspeakably fragile.'

VOTIVE LAMP

The Pope and the Sacred Heart
went off on the back of a cart,
and I've tried to find a home
for the Child of Prague.

If that lamp weren't the exact
shape of a brandy glass, there might be some chance
that I'd part with it.

Small chance, though.

If I'd been brought up in the clear light
of reason,
I might feel differently.

But I often come home in the dark

and, from the hall door,
in the red glow
I can discern
a child's violin
and, coming closer,
a plover;
the photograph of a dead friend;
three hazelnuts gathered from a well;
and three leather-skinned shamans
who flew all the way from Asia
on one card.

I designed none of this and don't know whether
sacred objects and images tend to cluster
around a constant light,
or whether
the small star's constancy,
through other lives and other nights,
now confers some sanctity
on my life's bric-a-brac.

CRANNÓG

Where an ash bush grows in the lake
a ring of stones has broken cover
in this summer's drought.
Not high enough to be an island,
it holds a disc of stiller water
in the riffled lake.

Trees have reclaimed the railway line behind us;
behind that, the road goes east —
as two lines parallel in space and time run away from us
this discovered circle draws us in.
In drowned towns
bells toll only for sailors and for the credulous
but this necklace of wet stones,
remnant of a wattle Atlantis,
catches us all by the throat.

We don't know what beads or blades
are held in the bog lake's wet amber
but much of us longs to live in water
and we recognise this surfacing
of old homes of love and hurt.

A troubled bit of us is kin
to people who drew a circle in water,
loaded boats with stone,
and raised a dry island and a fort
with a whole lake for a moat.

SHARDS

My garden is a graveyard for plates and cups
or else there's a bull in a china shop at the earth's core.
Each year's digging draws up a new hoard
and there's democracy in all the brokenness.
A blue pagoda lands next to a dandelion;
heavy delft and rosy wedding china
are beaten bright by the same May rain.
All equal now in the brown loam,
not all saw equal service or were mourned equally,
yet not one fragment gives anything away,
not a word of all they heard or saw,
or of the hands which used them roughly or with care —
dumb witnesses of hungers sated and thirsts slaked,
of the rare chances of communion,
before they were broken, and returned,
clay to clay,
having been through the fire
and having been a vessel for a while.

INTRODUCTIONS
for Brendan and Ursula Flynn

Some of what we love
we stumble upon —
a purse of gold thrown on the road,
a poem, a friend, a great song.

And more
discloses itself to us —
a well among green hazels,
a nut thicket —
when we are worn out searching
for something quite different.

And more
comes to us, carried
as carefully
as a bright cup of water,
as new bread.

MURDERING THE LANGUAGE

Why did I love
the neat examination of a noun under the pointer,
the analysis of a sentence lifted out of talk,
canal water halted in a lock?

Mood, tense, gender.
What performs the action,
What suffers the action?
What governs what?
What qualifies, modifies?

When we whispered in our desks
we spoke our book of invasions —
an unruly wash of Victorian pedantry,
Cromwellian English, Scots,
the jetsam and the beached bones of Irish —
a grammarian's nightmare.

But we parsed a small rectangular sea
and never missed the flow
or wondered why victories won in blood
are fastened in grammar
and in grammar's dream of order;
or why the dream of order draws us
as surely as the dream of freedom
or why correct language is spoken only in the capital.

Our language was tidal;
it lipped the quartzite cliffs,
a long and tedious campaign,
and ran up the beaches, over sand, seaweed, stones.

Laws learned by heart in school are the hardest to unlearn,
but too much has been suffered since
in the name of who governs whom.
It is time to step outside the cold schools,
to find a new, less brutal grammar
which can allow what we know:
that this northern shore was wrought
not in one day, by one bright wave,
but by tholing the rush and tug of many tides.

HUNTER'S MOON

There are, perhaps, no accidents,
no coincidences.
When we stumble against people, books,
rare moments out of time,
these are illuminations —
like the hunter's moon
that sails tonight in its high clouds,
casting light into our black harbour,
where four black turf boats
tug at their ropes,
hunger for the islands.

ONTARIO DRUMLIN

Having run out the boat,
what stop of the heart
causes us to beach on the half-known
as Colmcille dragged up his skin boat
on the white strand of Iona?
An exile surely,
but the same salt-shriven grass,
the same wind at his heels.

Or what in me longs enough for the diminutive
in a continent of trees,
for this name to grip
here beside the Otonabee?

Druimlín,
little back, little hill,
a glacier kernel
rounded and stony
as any in Ulster's Cavan,
though the trees on it are red
and the hill's real name
is not heard.

PATCHED KAYAK

Royal Ontario Museum, Toronto

Who made the parchment boat?
Who bent and bound ribs of drifted wood
to a long clean frame?
Who stretched sealskins,
plaited sinew,
stitched the stitches?
Which mapped the making,
which mapped the wounds,
which curved along the edges of the lives of seals,
the edges of the lives of women,
the edges of the lives of men.

OYSTERS

There is no knowing,
or hardly any,
more wondering —
for no one knows what joy the stone holds
in its stone heart,
or whether the lark is full of sorrow
as it springs against the sky.
What do we know, for instance,
of the ruminations of the oyster
which lies on the estuary bed —
not the rare, tormented pearl-maker,
just the ordinary oyster?
Does it dream away its years?

Or is it hard,
this existence where salt and river water mix?
The endless filtering
to sustain a pale silky life,
the labouring to build a grey shell,
incorporating all that floods and tides push in its way,
stones, mud, the broken shells of other fish.

Perhaps the oyster does not dream or think or feel at all
but then how can we understand
the pull of that huge muscle beside the heart
which clamps the rough shell shut
before a hunting starfish or a blade
but which opens it
to let in the tide?

TENDING

When a wood fire burns down and falls apart
the fire in each log dies quickly
unless burnt ends are tilted together —
a moment's touch, recognition;
gold and blue flame
wraps the singing wood.

VIOLIN

Wherever music comes from
it must come through an instrument.
Perhaps that is why we love the instrument best
which is most like us —

a long neck,
a throat that loves touch,
gut,
a body that resonates,

and life, the bow of hair and wood
which works us through the necessary cacophonous hours,
which welds dark and light into one deep tone,
which plays us, reluctant, into music.

VIOLA D'AMORE

Sometimes love does die,
but sometimes, a stream on porous rock,
it slips down into the inner dark of a hill,
joins with other hidden streams
to travel blind as the white fish that live in it.
It forsakes one underground streambed
for the cave that runs under it.
Unseen, it informs the hill,
and, like the hidden strings of the *viola d'amore*,
makes the hill reverberate,
so that people who wander there
wonder why the hill sings,
wonder why they find wells.

ARCTIC TERN

Love has to take us unawares
for none of us would pay love's price if we knew it.
For who will pay to be destroyed?
The destruction is so certain,
so evident.

Much harder to chart,
less evident,
is love's second life,
a tern's egg,
revealed and hidden
in a nest of stones
on a stony shore.

What seems a stone
is no stone.
This vulnerable pulse
which could be held in the palm of a hand
may survive
to voyage the world's warm and frozen oceans,
its tapered wings,
the beat of its small heart,
a span between arctic poles.

MILK

Could he have known
that any stranger's baby
crying out loud in a street
can start the flow?
A stain that spreads
on fustian
or denim.

This is kindness
which in all our human time
has refused to learn propriety,
which still knows nothing
but the depth of kinship,
the depth of thirst.

WINTER PATHS

There is something about winter
which pares all living things down to their essentials —
a bare tree,
a black hedge,
hold their own stark thrones in our hearts.

Once, after searching a valley,
summer after summer,
I went in winter
and found, at last, the path
that linked the well to the little roofless churches —
a crooked way through fields.
Leafless, fruitless, the briar-bound stone walls
revealed their irregular gaps —
the way cattle and goats
and women and men
had passed, winter after winter,
drawing aside or shoving past stray strands of briar,
wondering if they'd know their way again in summer.

HAZELNUTS

I thought that I knew what they meant
when they said that wisdom is a hazelnut.
You have to search the scrub
for hazel thickets,
gather the ripened nuts,
crack the hard shells,
and only then taste the sweetness at wisdom's kernel.

But perhaps it is simpler.
Perhaps it is we who wait in thickets
for fate to find us
and break us between its teeth
before we can start to know anything.

MOUNTAIN

Beauty can ambush us, even through a car window.
This green galleon sails eternally through Sligo,
dragging our hearts in its wake.

One singer was found by hunters on these green flanks
and another chose them as a deep cradle for his bones
but neither the Fianna's chroniclers nor Yeats
did more than pay their respects
to what was already here —

a mountain
which had already
shaken off glaciers,
carried a human cargo,
known grace in stone.

It might have been the same February light
on these tender slopes
which drew the first people from the coast
to set their fires on this plateau,
to build on this great limestone boat
whose boards are made of fishbones,
whose water is green time.

CORRIE

On the lake's lip
under this year's scribbles —
Phil and Fiona Feb 96 —
scores in red sandstone
show
where the glacier passed.

Having quarried out
the mountain's core,
it abandoned blocks of rock
at the valley's neck,
carried and scattered the rest
as it went down,
ground it into boulders,
red pebbles,
sand,

left behind
a bowl
of light.

SCRÍOB

Start again from nothing and scrape
since scraping is now part of us;
the sheep's track, the plough's track
are marked into the page,
the pen's scrape cuts a path on the hill.

But today I brought back
three bones of a bird,
eaten before it was hatched
and spat or shat out with its own broken shell
to weather on the north cliffs of Hoy.

This is an edge
where the pen runs dumb.
The small bleached bones of a fulmar or gannet
have nothing to tell.
They have known neither hunger nor flight
and have no understanding of the darkness
which came down and killed.

Tracks run to an end,
sheep get lost in the wet heather.
There are things which can neither be written, nor spoken,
nor read;
thin wing bones which cannot be mended.

Too fragile for scraping,
the bones hold in their emptiness
the genesis of the first blown note.

THOLE-PIN

Who speaks of victory? Endurance is all.
Rainer Maria Rilke

Words, old tackle,
obsolete tools
moulder in outhouses, sheds of the mind —
the horse-collar rots on a high hook;
a flat-iron and an open razor rust together.

Sometimes a word is kept on
at just one task, its hardest,
in the corner of some trade or skill.
Thole survives,
a rough dowel
hammered into a boat's gunnel
to endure,
a pivot
seared between elements.

EASTER HOUSES

During the last weeks of Lent
our play was earnest.
We'd hack sods out of the grass
and stack them among the trees
into four low walls.
The Easter house never had a roof —
what we needed was a place
where we could boil eggs outside.

After the battened-up heart of winter,
the long fast of spring,
life had come out again to nest in the open;
again, the shell was chipped open from within.

SONG IN WINDSOR, ONTARIO

Ice whispers
as it crushes against
steelbound, staggering timbers
in the Detroit river.

Great plates of ice from the lakes
catch on the banks,
turn under the March sun,
crumple each other
to show
how mountain ranges are made.

And on the wooden pylons,
a small bird
is back with the seed of music,
two notes,
the interval of desire
registered on the stirring cities.

DRIVING THROUGH LIGHT IN WEST LIMERICK

> *Poetry,*
> *Exceeding music, must take the place*
> *Of empty heaven and its hymns.*
> Wallace Stevens

What's light that falls on nothing?
Nothing.
But this light turns wet trees into green lamps
and roadside grass into a green blaze
and lets the saffron hills run through our hearts
as though the world had no borders
and wet whin bushes were deeper than the sun.

What's light,
and who can hold it?
This morning, across the sea, in a gallery
I saw light held for five hundred years
on an angel's face —
a moment's surprise,
and centuries fell away
quiet as leaves.

But the angel's features
had been no more than any perfect features
until they'd caught the light
or else the light had fallen on them.

And trying to figure out
which had happened
I got off the Underground at King's Cross
and an accordion tune filled
the deep steel stairwell.

This was some descent of the strong sun,
good music
brought down to where it was needed,
music, surpassing poetry,
gone down again,
the busker with a red *Paolo Soprani*
telling again
of Orpheus in Connacht.

The escalators ground up and down
carrying all the people
up and down a hill
of saffron light.

ISOLDE'S TOWER, ESSEX QUAY

It is our fictions which make us real.
Robert Kroetsch

Is there no end
to what can be dug up
out of the mud of a riverbank,

no end
to what can be dug up
out of the floodplains of a language?

This is no more
than the sunken stump
of a watchtower on a city wall,
built long after any Isolde might have lived,
built over since a dozen times,
uncovered now in some new work —
a tower's old root in black water
behind a Dublin bus stop;

And the story is no more than a story.
Tristan drifted in here on the tide to be healed,
taken in because of his music,
and a long yarn spun on
of which they'd say —

> 'Had not the lovers of whom this story tells
> Endured sorrow for the sake of love
> They would never have comforted so many.'

ATTENTION

Sometimes there is nothing,
absolutely nothing,
to be done but watch
and wait
and let the clock which breaks our days
let go its grasp
until the mind is able
to trust the storm
to bear up our weight of flesh and bone
to take on the time of breath
the rhythm of blood
a rhythm held
between two breaths
a bright cry
a last rasp.

AN ALTERED GAIT

With the scurry of a sandpiper
a gull runs and runs along the tideline.
It trails something dark behind it,
the broken rim
of its right wing.

A fortnight ago
as my father lay dying
he sometimes lifted his good right arm,
the same troubled eye —
the same hurry told in his breath
as we waited
and he laboured
towards the flight out.

BULBS

I put them down late, in November,
into the grass of the cold garden.
It is hard to believe that they will grow at all
or that the brown papery onions,
now stowed in the ground,
have life in them.

Yet before the frosts are finished
they will come up,
green spears through the grass,
like sleeping legions returning in our time of need.
That time is spring,
when courage is necessary and scarce,
when each green blade will break and yield up
last summer's hoarded sun.

NIGHT

Coming back from Cloghane
in the sudden frost
of a November night,
I was ambushed
by the river of stars.

Disarmed by lit skies
I had utterly forgotten
this arc of darkness,
this black night
where the frost-hammered stars
were notes thrown from a chanter,
crans of light.

So I wasn't ready
for the dreadful glamour of Orion
as he struck out over Barr dTrí gCom
in his belt of stars.

At Gleann na nGealt
his bow of stars
was drawn against my heart.

What could I do?
Rather than drive into a pitch-black ditch
I got out twice,
leaned back against the car
and stared up at our windy, untidy loft
where old people had flung up old junk
they'd thought might come in handy,
ploughs, ladles, bears, lions, a clatter of heroes,
a few heroines, a path for the white cow, a swan
and, low down, almost within reach,
Venus, completely unfazed by the frost.

MIGRATIONS

The strong geese claim the sky again
and tell and tell and tell us
of the many shifts and weathers
of the long-boned earth.

Blind to their huge, water-carved charts,
our blood dull to the tug of poles,
we are tuned still to the rising and dying of light
and we still share their need
to nest and to journey.

BETWEEN THE JIGS AND THE REELS

Between a jig and a reel
what is there?
Only one beat
escaped from a ribcage.

Tunes are migratory
and fly from heart to heart
intimating
that there's a pattern
to life's pulls and draws.

Because what matters to us most
can seldom be told in words
the heart's moods are better charted
in its own language —

the rhythm of Cooley's accordion
which could open the heart of a stone,
John Doherty's dark reels
and the tune that the sea taught him,
the high parts of the road and the underworlds
which only music and love can brave
to bring us back to our senses
and on beyond.

III
CARRYING THE SONGS

(2007)

WINTER BIRDS

I have frequently seen, with my own eyes, more than a thousand of these
small birds hanging down on the sea-shore from one piece of timber,
enclosed in their shells and already formed.
Giraldus Cambrensis, *Topographia Hibernica*

From the cliffs of Northern Greenland
the black-breasted geese come down
to graze on the wind-bitten sedges of Inis Cé.
They land in October, exhausted,
bringing with them their almost-grown young.

No one on these shores could ever find their nests,
so in early times it was concluded
that they had hatched from the pupa-shaped goose barnacle —
as fish, they were eaten on Fridays.

In April they gather now, restless, broody,
fatted on the scant grasses of a continent's margin,
ready to leave for breeding grounds in Greenland's tundra.

Watching that nervous strut and clamour —
a tuning orchestra raucous before the signal
to rise on the wind
in a harmony
old as hunger —
the name grips somewhere else,
my father's talk of 'winter-birds' in his class
in South Donegal,
the name his schoolmaster had given
to big boys and girls

who sat in the back seats,
back from the Lagan,
bound soon for Scotland,
already seasoned,
their migratory patterns set.

CARRYING THE SONGS
for Tríona and Maighread Ní Dhomhnaill

Those in power write the history, those who suffer write the songs
Frank Harte

It was always those with little else to carry
who carried the songs
to Babylon,
to the Mississippi —
some of these last possessed less than nothing
did not own their own bodies
yet, three centuries later,
deep rhythms from Africa,
stowed in their hearts, their bones,
carry the world's songs.

For those who left my county,
girls from Downings and the Rosses
who followed herring boats north to Shetland
gutting the sea's silver as they went
or boys from Ranafast and Horn Head
who took the Derry boat,
who slept over a rope in a bothy,
songs were their souls' currency,
the pure metal of their hearts,

to be exchanged for other gold,
other songs which rang out true and bright
when flung down
upon the deal boards of their days.

TIMBRE

A word does not head out alone.
It is carried about the way something essential,
a blade, say, or a bowl,
is brought from here to there
when there is work to be done.
Sometimes, after a long journey,
it is pressed into a different service.

A tree keeps its record
of the temper of years
well hidden.

After the timber has been sawn
rough rings release the song of the place —
droughts, good summers, long frosts —
the way pain and joy unlock in a voice.

OUR WORDS

Our words are cart-ruts
back into our guttural histories;
they are rabbit-tracks, printed
into the morning snow on a headland;
they are otter runs,
urgent between fresh and salt water;
they are dunlin tracks at the tide's edge.
They will be erased by the next wave
but, in the meantime, they assure us
that we are not alone
and that we are heirs to all the treasure
which words have ever netted.

Abetted by trade winds,
they cross channels, oceans.
Seeds in the mud of a soldier's boot,
they come ashore, part, at first,
of an arrogant, hobnailed scrape,
language of the rough-tongued *guerrier.*

But time does forgive them,
almost forgives them conquest —
Hard slangs of the market-place
are ground down to pillow-talk
and, as the language of conquest
grows cold in statute books,
elsewhere, its words are subsumed
into the grammars of the conquered

'I be, you be, he bees.'

The new words are golden, glamorous.
Grown old, they are dark pennies,
old friends to oxtercog us home.

And although so many
will be wiped out by the next wave,
we will never run short
because a mill on the ocean floor grinds them out,
keeping the tongue salt.

FIRST POETRY
for Henry and Deirdre Comerford

These were, perhaps, the original poetry,
swallows, terns, or grey-lag geese,
returning, unnoticed at first,
over the sea's rim,
or through the same dip in the hills,
in tune with the lift and fall of the seasons,
returning from nowhere,
or from an unknown terrain
which must consequently exist —

    the warm countries,
    the frozen regions,
    the isles of the blest,
    Indies of the mind.

They needed, for no obvious reason, two worlds
in which to feed and breed,
so they needed a capacity for sustained flight,
a fine orientation,
an ability to sleep on the wing
an instinct for form and its rhythms
as each took its turn to cut the wind.

As they flocked or spelled their way high over April
they needed hunger, and faith
and vital grace.

FORGETTING TULIPS
  for Brídín and Kathleen

Today, on the terrace, he points with his walking-stick and asks
'What do you call those flowers?'

On holiday in Dublin in the sixties
he bought the original five bulbs for one pound.
He planted and manured them for thirty-five years.
He lifted them, divided them,
stored them on chicken wire in the shed,
ready for planting in a straight row,
high red and yellow cups —

treasure transported in galleons
from Turkey to Amsterdam, three centuries earlier.
In April they sway now, in a Donegal wind,
above the slim leaves of sleeping carnations.

A man who dug straight drills and picked blackcurrants,
who taught rows of children parts of speech,
tenses and declensions
under a cracked canvas map of the world —
who loved to teach the story
of Marco Polo and his uncles arriving home,
bedraggled after ten years' journeying,
then slashing the linings of their coats
to spill out rubies from Cathay —

today, shedding the nouns first,
he stands by his flowerbed and asks,
'What do you call those flowers?'

AUGERS

There were rusted augers scattered about the house,
ancestors of the brace-barrel and the electric drill,
owned by the old electrician who had lived here before me.
He was the youngest apprentice, perhaps, in a scratched photo
of the Galway Electrical Company, 1910 —
the boy in a baggy, flat cap, seated, cross-legged,
in front of older working-men,
all grimly yet gamely posed,
a crew embarking to illuminate dark streets.
I kept the largest auger as a poker for the range,
kept it for luck,
investing it with a sense of augury.

Last summer I heard of a second set of augers.
When my Erskine grand-uncles, the last three,
left Kilcar for Chicago,
their four siblings gone before them,
they pulled the door closed behind them,
not bothering to lock it.

Their valuables had been left with neighbours
who, three-quarters of a century later,
returned them to my cousin —
a bundle of augers for fixing boats.

Seven Edward Erskines had fished off the same white strand
since the first one had come from Scotland
and had married in.

He had hardly brought the augers with him,
but the word was already well travelled,
essential gear, tucked away in the holds of many boats,
having navigated northern coasts, centuries,
having tested the grain of languages, dialects —
Nafarr, nafogār, nave-gār, auger, boat-spear.

DEMOLITION

On the gable of the adjoining house
at first-floor level, high above the people running to work
a rectangular black smudge shows where the range used to be.
To the left of the smudge,
there is a recess with six shelves.
On the fourth shelf up is half a bag of self-raising flour
with the top folded down.
Below it are a tin of Royal Baking Powder
and a glass salt cellar.

And something about this hurts badly
but I don't know what
or why I now remember waking at four in the morning,
long ago, the day after a love ended abruptly,
feeling that the room had no walls,
and that the winds of the world blew across my bed
and that I had no shelter
or hope of shelter.

It's strange that in this exposed, vanished house,
it's not the bedroom walls with their ripped, primrose wallpaper
and their little fireplaces which bother me,
but the sliced-off kitchen,
the abandonment
of leaven and savour.

OUGHTERARD LEMONS

In Paup Joyce's garden in the nineteen-sixties
in a council estate called The Lemon Fields,
it is said that there was a bush
with small lemons growing on it.

An O'Flaherty of Aughanure Castle
had once shipped the trees from Spain
and had planted his land with them.

Stranger things had rooted,
had almost gone native —
tubers from the Americas some voyager had brought back —
so why not this counterpoint to honey,
like honey, a love-child of the sun.

A whiff of spice roads
and we drag dreams home from our journeys —
necessary evidence of other climates,
other ways of growing —

and some dreams do take root in the quotidian,
as surely as fuchsia rampages along a side-road,
and some dreams sustain us totally, then fail us totally

and some hardly take at all
but survive in the tang of a placename,
in a crazy bush tilted by the wind.

GOLDEN LANE

After a Christmas of rain and gales
there are four bright days
one after the other
at the start of January.

Across the lit milk of the bay
the sun hammers a path from Black Head to the prom,
a golden lane fit for any god
of winter, or light, or life
and strong enough for three teenagers in red jackets,
their arms held wide,
to play at walking out over the tide,
into the sun's heart.

Today it feels likely
that this is where early stonemasons,
who built tombs
with shafts to channel midwinter light,
marked the day that the sun stopped falling,
discovered that light at its lowest is most intense.

This early, winter's evening it feels likely
that the sun's habits were first charted,
not on land,
but on a bright arm of the sea
which illumined the path
of a low sun returning.

INDIGO

The indigo ridge
behind Benlettery horseshoe —

in late October light
it cut the early evening sky
and then the mountains fell down, down,
into deep Lough Inagh
and my heart
travelled the whole height and depth of them.

RÚN

An trí rud is sciobtha san fharraige, an rón, an roc agus an ronnach.
(The three fastest things in the sea, the seal, the ray and the mackerel.)
Gaelic, traditional

Sudden as a cormorant
the black head broke
through the silk of the morning estuary,
turned,
and swam near enough to the pier
for me to see two soft dents.

It watched for a long time,
curious
and silent,
against the grind of building sites,
the clatter and scrape of the docks,
the uneven hum of cars.

Then it tossed its nose in the air
and sank, on its back, down into its own world.
Before that I hadn't known that they were here.
Afterwards I'd stop and watch the channel for them.
A shimmer of rattled foil
showed that one was coming up
or had just gone.

Sometimes one would whack the water with its hind flippers
and leap up
leaving a brightness in my day,
so that I felt grateful
that it had stopped fishing
long enough to observe our frenzy
and somehow, to calm it.
Then, one day, further west,
I saw a colony of them,
warm slugs clustered on the seaward side of a rock —
one of the three fastest creatures in the sea,
one of the slowest and most awkward on land.

Their sea-black pelts
had turned golden in the sun
and I realised
how much they need this element too.
This is where they breed.
This is where they breathe.

STARLINGS

Some things can't be caught in words,
starlings over an October river, for instance —
the way they lift from a roof-ridge in a cloud
directed by a hidden choreographer;
the way they rise, bank and fall,
tugging at some uncharted artery of the human heart;
the way the cloud tilts, breaks and melds,
the undersides of wings garnering all the light
that's left in an evening sky;
the way they flow down onto a warehouse roof,
bird by brown bird.

BRIGHT CITY

I follow the morning light down the canal path,
across the road and on to the Claddagh.
In light which has turned canal, river and estuary to mercury,
even the cars on the Long Walk are transfigured.

Five swans beat their way in past the mud dock,
heavy, sounding their own clarion,
carrying the world's beauty
in on their strong white backs this Saturday morning.

STRANGER

After a week of walking
the angled streets and the hills
of the small city, with its towers and steel ships,
I wanted to be near a well.

And out past Dungarvan, I found one —
well-minded,
gravelled, full and quick.

The gale-driven rains of the past week
poured into the corner of it.
The hill was a pitcher
tilted forever
to fill
a worn stone cup.

WALKING OUT TO ISLAND EDDY
for Carol Langstaff and Jim Rooney

At low spring tide in February, when the wind is right,
the moon hauls the sea back off the sand bar for an hour or two,
allowing us to walk out to an island of roofless houses.

We have stumbled down over wrack-draped stones
and have waited, as, yard by yard,
a warm arm of sand rises out of the tide.

We wade the first few yards,
water lapping to the tops of our wellingtons,
and come up onto a road
of coarse, gold-and-indigo sand
and purple scallop fans.
Sarah says, 'This is how the Israelites crossed the Red Sea.
They must have known the tides.'

Behind us, a man, his grown son
and a dog have been driving
a flock of black-faced sheep along the grassline.
Now, they head them down,
through pools, bladderwrack and kelp.

One sheep is handled through the last of the ebbing tide.
The others scatter, bleating,
but are gathered up and herded
onto their sea-path, their path to summer grass.

We stand aside to let them pass.

Their hooves crush and crush loudly into the seabed
as they trot between the upright flutes of razor shells
and the tiny, breath-driven geysers of the clams.

SHEEP AT NIGHT IN THE INAGH VALLEY
for Leo and Clare

Maybe the dry margins draw them,
or grass, sprouting among limestone chippings —
they are here, as always,
on the edge of the tarmac
on a bend.

They shelter under clumped rushes —
white bundles in the night —
their eyes are low green stars,
caught in the trawl of my car's headlights.

Occasionally one hirples across the road
but, usually, they stay put
and gaze at the slowed-down car.

I envy them their crazy trust.

WEANING

He carried a lamb
up over the bog to the hill,
took sugar from his pocket and let it lick.

The clean tongue searched the crevices of his hand,
then he set it down to graze.
It would never stray from that hill,
tethered by a dream of sweet grass.

WHIN

Before we'd heard of Van Gogh
we'd felt the hit of that yellow
when all the worst fields were rough-brushed,
overrun with a coconut-scented bush.

Barbed saffron, it trumpeted summer.
To farmers, it was a bright curse,
its rootball so tough and springy,
my father, as a boy, had cut sliotars from it.

In May, it lit hills and headlands;
brash, it invaded the earth —
'I'd know you on a whin bush in Australia'
was said to someone unexpectedly met.

But how were we supposed to greet
in fifth or sixth class when we did, at last, meet
the English language's only synonym —
furze and gorse, those lonely, identical twins.

BARBARI

Steering west through Barnes Gap, beyond Termon,
the granite hills fill the radio with hail,
obliterating Mozart
as they used obliterate the Sunday match.

West of here,
for the eighteenth-century traveller,
lay the Wilds of Donegal,
wild as Africa, but wetter.

From our side,
when I was a child,
an elderly neighbour told me
of a story he had heard as a child,

of a father from Horn Head,
coming to the door
to counsel his sons
as they headed east for Scotland.

'— Be yiz good boys now,
and once yiz go beyond Barnes Gap
take every man for a rogue.'

TO COLMCILLE RETURNING

It's time now to dig down
through the shingle of Port a' Churaich,
to bring up the skeleton of ash and oak,
to stretch new skins over the ribs
and to turn the beak of your boat to the south-west.

For this time your journey must be,
not across the spine of Britain
but across the scarred back of Ulster,
across the Sperrins and into the Glens
down through the Mournes and Sliabh Gullion
and into the small rainy towns with their supermarkets,
their video stores and graveyards,
into all the farms with their sprayed barns and Land Rovers,
their certainties
and their hurt.

You'll make your landfall at Derry,
Maiden City of the Planter,
oak grove of Cenél Conaill
in the territory of Cenél nEóghain —
citadel or sanctuary,
it was always half-beleaguered
the Foyle water north, east and south of it,
and, to the west,
'a bogge most uncommonlie wette'.

And this time you may take off the blindfold
for your vision is needed
and we'll need every ounce of your diplomacy,
you, who, in the middle of the path,
turned your back on much of what was native
and started out again
away from the carnage under Ben Bulben
and all your self-righteousness over the book,
you, who turned contrariness to grace
and scooped honey from the lion's skull.

GOING FOR MILK

Coming on the *Stop* sign at night
on the bend of a side street,
I braked too fast,
too far from the barrier.

The soldier with the red torch
and the machine-gun
stepped back,
spoke to someone in the steel tower
then half-circled the southern car.

'You'll be all right,
They won't do you a bit of harm if you don't scare them.'

Every morning before school
I took the can,
crossed the road,
climbed into McGarvey's field,
stepped down sideways from the bottom step
to avoid the mud
and turned a corner behind Barlows'
to where cows lifted their horns out of the long grass,
started to move in.

'Keep on going, they are far more afraid of you
than you are of them.'

The soldier at the car window has a helmet too big for him,
is barely an adult, seventeen, eighteen maybe,
younger than my nephew, smaller.
He smiles, in relief.

Who sent him out?
Who sent any of them out,
telling them once more
absent-mindedly, maybe,
turning off the TV
or hanging a cup up on a hook,

'They are all the same, that crowd,
trust none of them —
they're all tarred with the same brush.'
And who is going to tell them the truth
which is not simple,
which sounds like the blackest lie
when they have stood in a kitchen
where killing was done —

'They're not all the same.
Most of them are far more afraid of you
than you are of them.'

Be careful now,
but go on over, the milk is needed.

SCRIPT

The double line of prints
showed where a pup had dragged itself up
a few yards above the tidemark.
It panted, blinking away the driven sand,
while a wind-ripped tide ebbed fast.

A few other November strays
arrived to taste the end of the gale —
a couple in blue raincoats, down for the weekend,
and two boys on bikes who'd heard the news.

Rested now, maybe, or scared,
it took off down the long white beach,
its blubbery weight gallumphing
as it pulled itself up and forward on its front flippers,
building up speed
until its flesh rippled and it was carried
as much by rhythm as by strength,
like the statues on Easter Island,
like ourselves.

It stopped, its sides heaving,
as if the small, grey-spotted body might burst
but gathered itself and set off
collapsing again, yards short of the water.

After a long time it raised its head,
hauled itself down the last slope of sand,
through the first thin broken waves, into its own depth
and then there was nothing
but the winter sea
and a double row of prints.

We walked down the shore for a closer look.
Dug hard into the sand,
claw-marks
recorded a breast-stroke,
a perfect, cursive script
which reached
the ocean's lip.

SHELLS

We used to hunker on the Silver Strand,
sifting the shells after a storm,
hunting for cowries.

The pink, furled nuggets were stored in jam jars,
hoarded in jacket pockets, on windowsills,
with pelicans' feet,
razor shells,
scallop shells,
turret shells
and the rare, white wentletrap.

Ignorant of how Venus had sailed ashore,
we were already intrigued
by all the felt asymmetries
of the small sea-beasts' growth,
all the dizzy architecture
of the first flesh.

SURVIVORS

This morning, at Catherine's Island,
the sea-potatoes are strewn along the tideline
like stranded souls.
Shorn of their soft, brown spines,
they are pieces of sea-porcelain.

Some are smaller than a fingernail,
others big as a baby's fist —
the sea's whitework,
translucent, nearly heart-shaped,
their innards freighted with sand.

I lift one to admire its pinpoint symmetries
and it falls apart —
I rinse another in the tide
and it falls apart —

but yesterday they rode out a North Atlantic gale
which churned the sea-bed, dug them up,
trundled them along in the roots of waves,
until their spines were worn off,
then swept them up here, on tufts of foam —

an impossibly safe landing
for frail coats of bone.

BREASTBONE

The loop of collar-bone is intact,
anchored still with sinew
to a perfect wind-keel;
the ribs are hollow straws;
the skewed shoulder-blades are thrown back
in the long curves of helmet-wings.

When I found it on the sand at Killehoey
it was already white,
clean of meat.

Light from the street
falls through its grained ivory
onto a page.

Nothing we make is as strong
or as light
as this.

EXUBERANCE
i.m. Fergal O Connor

In the heatwave of seventy-six,
the year of our finals,
we tried to study opposite the library,
scorching ourselves by the square lake.
As students loped past
in frayed Levi's and cheesecloth shirts
we read Plato and Locke, Mill and Marx —
a palimpsest of world maps,
each one cancelling the last.
We drank coffee and talked
and fell awkwardly in and out of love.
Where, if anywhere, was truth?

The following summer, in County Louth
in the abandoned garden of Castle Roche
an exuberance of medieval herbs was found,
a physic garden, which had germinated
in the previous year's deep heat.
Possibly the herbs had come up often,
unrecorded by botanists,
unobserved among dandelions and docks.

Or possibly not — beside a sarcophagus,
in the Valley of the Kings
a bowl of wheat grains was found.
Three millennia after they had been entombed
to ensure nourishment in the next world,
some good grains were carried back
and they grew
in the moisture and the light of our time.

BANNY

'As a child in Tyrone you'd be told
to banny the cat, to stroke it gently.
I suppose it comes from *beannaigh*,' she says.

She uses the word for the first time in eighty years, maybe,
as she rhythmically blesses her own old cat,
in its own tactile, enduring vernacular.

.

ORIENTATION

*We must go on groping from one illusion of virtue to another; the fact is
that man cannot act at all without moral impulse, however mistaken...*
Arthur Miller

A flock of seagulls
rocks on the water
at the sheltered end of Nimmo's pier —
the birds' white breasts all turned into the January wind.

Crystals in cooling magma
orient themselves to magnetic north
as towards a constant
although, over deep time,
poles shift about like bedrock or stars.

For us, who carry,
in our twined chromosomes,
all the wonder and terror
evolved within animal time and bone —

the carnage of our last century
and of the century just begun —
for us, might there be
some wandering pole or orient,

towards which some primal grain in us
might align itself, some kind of good,
some love, not absolutely constant,

but, within the time which comprehends us,
constant enough to draw us
like these seagulls, their tails and bills
the dipping points of compass needles.

AUBADE

Every morning, this clear, February week,
at ten-to-seven, I've been drawn out of sleep
by this rich note —
far better than any rooster —
and such a strong song
from such a small,
black bird.

I wondered if the boiler had jolted him
out of his own dreams
and I re-timed it to see
but, bang-on ten-to-seven,
he was giving out the pay
from near the top of the apple tree,
lit up at another dawn
and quite oblivious that his song
was erasing my guilt
regarding last autumn's great crop
which had lain rotting,
pecked hollow,
and rocking in the grass,
unbaked, unbottled,
or so I had thought.

POLLEN

And this dust survives
through the deaths of ages.
It sleeps in deep layers of mud —
black, red and umber;
it sleeps under the wet pelt of a November hill
where long grass is the colour of fox;
it sleeps deep under lakes;
twelve metres down it survives,
dust of arctic meadows,
old and tough
as love.

VOGELHERD HORSE, 30,000 BC

Art, it would seem, is born like a foal that can walk straight away.
John Berger

The horse is half the length
of my little finger —
cut from mammoth ivory
its legs have been snapped off,
three at the haunch,
the fourth above the knee
but its neck, arched as a Lippizaner's,
its flared nostrils,
are taut with life.

The artist or shaman who carved it
as totem, ornament or toy
could hardly have envisioned
that horses would grow tall,
would be bridled, saddled,
that of all the herds of mammoths,
lords of the blond steppes,
not one animal would survive,
that the steppes would dwindle,
that, in the stacked mountains to the south,
rivers would alter course

but that this horse would gallop on
across ten thousand years of ice,
would see the deaths, the mutations of species
would observe the burgeoning of one species,
Homo faber, the maker,
who had made him,
or, who, using a stone or bone knife,
had sprung him from the mammoth's tusk,
had buffed him with sand,
taking time with the full cheeks, the fine chin,
and had set him down on the uneven floor
of the Vogelherd cave
to ride time out.

CHAUVET

for John Berger

One red line, defining his rump,
draws the small mammoth out of the cave wall,
renders him more than a stalagmite.

In another chamber,
a bear's paw protrudes,
outlined in charcoal.

The animals had been in the wall all along,
awaiting recognition, release.
The Stone Age artists knew it,

just as the Italian master would know it,
as his chisel unlocked perfect forms
from Carrara's marble,

as we know it,
when some informed, deft gesture —
a tilt in a melody,

a lit line in a poem or a song —
draws us out into our humanity,
warm-blooded, bewildered.

THE FORCE

I used never notice this —
starlings rifling the ivy
for the last of last year's black fruit,
or green flames erupting
from the bronze bark of the apple tree.

I used to see primroses, all right —
warm banks of them
and fields of daffodils
in front of old people's houses,
and house-martins moulding mud nests
under the eaves —

but I never noticed the tall leaves of iris or montbretia
rise from the brown swirl of last year's withering,
or heard the roundness in the blackbird's throat —
I had no notion of that dogged, sullen power
which shoves up,
year after battered year,
as the earth's hot kernel
picks up its flagging conversation with the sun,

in a language of wingbeat
and pungent earth
and silk parting bark.

LAMPED

I had left Streedagh Strand behind me,
with the Atlantic white and rough in the October dusk
when it started to rise,
left of the Ox mountains.
First, it was a lit blip and then,
a silver lid lifting out of cloud.

As the Hunter's Moon shed
its last rigid wisp of cloud,
I steered north and it rode high to my right —
a lamp to guide or stun
night animals, insects, birds.

All the way north it held high
until, at Barnesmore Gap,
it lifted over the right-hand hill
and struck Lough Mourne across the middle,
struck it silver in the black bog.

I drew in on the grass
because this was the same as a moon lake
which I'd seen from a mountain top
as I was leaving childhood.

And here I was, once again,
lamped.

IV
HANDS

(2011)

SOUNDPOST
  for the Con Tempo String Quartet

'Its tone came from the soundpost —
it was made from a bird's bone.'
A musician tells of his friend's fiddle,
the one on which so many
well-shaped tunes
had been turned and played.

In French it is called *l'ame,*
the instrument's soul;
in Cremona, when the master-luthier
brought a supply of slow-growing timber
down from the high Alps,
to shape around his moulds,
it was called *la anima* —

a round peg of wood,
positioned carefully inside the instrument,
almost under the bridge,
to hold apart belly and back,
to gather every vibration of the strings,
every lift and fall of the bower's wrist,
to carry all that is in us of flight,
through the woods of the instrument.

REED-MAKING
for Cormac

Man is but a reed, the most feeble thing in nature, but he is a thinking reed.
Blaise Pascal

A strip of cane is whittled, gouged thin,
cut in two;
its concave sides are held together;
tapered ends bound, with waxed thread,
to a brass funnel,
then fitted into a chanter.

If one turns out well
and is played in
by a fine musician,
the lips of the reed
will come to vibrate in sympathy,
and all things will flow through them —
joy, grief, despair, and again, joy —
stories told in secret to a tree;
told to a reed;
carried back on a channel of air
into life's bright rooms.

What generates music?
Gouged, bound wood,
or wind, or breath,
playing on a tension between
what is bound and what is free —
a child blows on a grass blade held between two thumbs,
wind blows across the holes in a hollow steel gate,
and blood leaps in response —
a hare alerted in tall grass.

DRIVING BACK OVER THE BLUE RIDGE,

you say that the leaves are late in turning.
Halfway up the wooded hill to our right
the sun has decanted itself
into a single maple tree.

There are days like that
which sing orange and red
in the forest of our ordinary green.

These are the days we hang our souls upon
as, high above them, the sun withdraws.

OPENINGS

In my chest
a rusted metal door
is creaking open,
the door of a decompression chamber
cranked up on barnacled chains.

The rush of air hurts and hurts
as larks fly
in and out,
in and out
between my bended ribs.

STILL LIFE

Much though we love best
those intersections of time and space
where we are love's playthings,
a sweet anonymity of flesh —
life's blessed rhythm
loving itself through us,
two human bodies tuned
to the whirring stars —

this is almost nothing
without the small, quotidian gifts,
habitual caresses which hinder fears,
the grace of small services rendered —
two bowls of blueberries and yoghurt,
two cups of coffee,
two spoons,
laid out on a wooden table
in October sunlight.

the sun has come down the valley and
turned the house-slates silver;
rain and hail have come down the valley;
small trees have curved down to the river
and the poplars have stood tall
and only a little bare at the top.

Here and there, in the green cloud of birch and hazel
above the hermitage of Santa Eulalia,
a wild cherry tree sings russet
and the mountain tops around us are furred with trees.

The bare peaks far to the east
have captured a first fall of snow;
the trees and mountains carry on
as though nature had not been conquered;
the grass deepens towards evening
and the little scalloped slates shine in the dusk.

ONLY THE SHADOWS

show us what light is —
the hard shadows of poplars
on the valley's green, warm floor;
broken shadow in the forefront of a Pissarro painting,
as a young woman washes dishes outside in sunlight;
shadows in our lives — sickness, loss, death.

Shadows
alert our vision
to the living light in clear-blooded trees,
dappled light on blue and white cotton,
washed light on stacked vessels.

OCTOBER

In the very late morning,
the sun rolls up again
over a saddle in the high Pyrenees
and each roof in the village
is a slab of light.
The slated farmhouses
are grappled in tiers
onto the steep, south-facing
side of the valley, so that folded schist,
slate and marble insist
into the homes of humans upstairs
and into the homes of animals downstairs
and after heavy rain
little springs trickle in through the houses'
back rock-walls.

This morning,
each of those stone and slate houses,
warms up like a brick oven,
warms up like the small black cats
who cross the lanes of Farrera.
I sit at the east-facing kitchen window,
slicing fruit, drinking coffee and light
and sadness falls away from my shoulders.

VAL DE LUZ

Light fills every
poplar and ash leaf
in the valley;
fills the leaves of the wild cherry and the birch
which have laboured for months
to turn light and water
into life and fruit
and which wait now
to be paid in gold.

FARRERA LIGHT

Why should the evening sun
which blasts light through the tops
of the slender yellow poplars in the valley
and of the red wild cherry trees on the hillside;
which lingers, a fillet of light in the dusk,
on the green ridge slanting down
to the hermitage of Santa Eulalia;
which shafts, a slightly opened blue fan,
onto range upon fretted range
of peaks to the east,
why should it shaft me too
with unaccountable joy?

NO GOOD REASON

There is no good reason
why my heart should be so gladdened
by a green hillside which turns golden,
or by an echoing jangle of bells —
the mountain's many-hoofed glockenspiel —
or by the sight of the old, bow-legged shepherd
who, propped on his stick,
leans against his jeep and waits
for his son to bring down the flock.

HANDS

for Eamonn and Kathleen

It was somewhere over the north-eastern coast of Brazil,
over Fortaleza, a city of which I know nothing,
except that it is full of people —
the life of each one a mystery
greater than the Amazon —
it was there, as the toy plane on the flight monitor
nudged over the equator
and veered east towards Marrakech,
that I started to think again of hands,
of how strange it is that our lives —
the life of the red-haired French girl to my left,
the life of the Argentinian boy to my right,
my life, and the lives of all the dozing passengers,
who are being carried fast in the dark
over the darkened Atlantic —
all of these lives are now being held
in the hands of the pilot,
in the consciousness of the pilot,
and I think of other hands which can hold our lives,
the hands of the surgeon
whom I will meet again when I return home,
the hands of the black-haired nurse
who unwound the birth-cord from my neck,
the soft hands of my mother,
the hands of those others
who have loved me,
until it seems almost
as though this is what a human life is:
to be passed from hand to hand,
to be borne up, improbably, over an ocean.

ORCHIDS

Today the ward is filling up with orchids.
Beyond the pink terraced houses and the January trees
the clouds break apart
to illuminate curtain after curtain of grey hail,
which batter in fast across the bay.

And tall orchids,
have arrived
in the cancer wards —
magnificent as crinolined beauties,
at the ball
before a battle.

YESTERDAY I WAS LISTENING ON THE iPOD

to Vivaldi's cello concerto —
so I did not hear the helicopter land
below in the hospital yard
or see them carrying in two stretchers.

Two hours earlier, a young woman,
half my age,
had fallen into the Atlantic with her son.
A long, long fall from the cliff top —
in a car crash the bonnet crumples so slowly —
I wonder if time slowed down for them
as they plummeted past layers of limestone,
layers of mudstone,
layers of the earth's time?

I wonder what terrors had flayed her,
whether they cried out to the fleeing earth,
whether she held him in her arms,
or by the hand,
and I wonder whether
some strong-winged angel
caught them both by the wrist
as they entered the tide at the cliff's foot,
whether there was light and music
to meet them —

and, if not, I wonder
whether Vivaldi's music can be
a bright bridge to nowhere;
or whether all of us can be
falling down time's long cliff,
each of us alone,
with all our fears in our arms.

PARISII

My father was a Paris cattle man.
Dante Alighieri, *Purgatorio*

The Parisii, who ferried travellers
across this shallow bend of the river,
with its two islands —
unmatched as the eyes
of a Picasso demoiselle —
lived on a worn trade route
which led north to wintry islands,
south to an empire,
and an inland sea.

They knew little of the glitter and tramp
of the Roman legions
that would soon bear down on their homes;
nothing of northern longboats
that would rip the river with their oars
or of tanks that would motor in over metalled roads;
they knew nothing of Attila
or of Charlemagne;
nothing of cathedrals, like tethered ships,
of the flourish of baroque courts
or the hour of the *sans-culottes*,
nothing of painted canvas,
jazz, or of heated café talk,

but, waiting, on the wooden quays,
to load silver or cloth,
or casting off in their tapered cots,
raw-knuckled, in February frost and fog
they must have known this —
dawn raddling the grey river
which separated two parts of Gaul.

LITTLE SKELLIG
for Paul Cannon

It is not difficult to believe,
a little, in archangels here
as golden-headed gannets swoop
around our lurching boat.
They are poised
as spray-blown row upon row
of cherubim,
along the ledges
of a tooth of sandstone,
which, for centuries,
has been whitewashed with guano
until its galleries are luminous, clamorous
as New York or Singapore.

The boatman in his yellow coat
restarts the engine and twists for home.
Salt water sloshes across the deck
then one gannet plummets
and there is something
about the greed and grace
of that cruciform plunge
which shouts out
to our unfeathered bones.

SEA URCHINS

These distant cousins of starfish
are dug into their hard honeycomb above the tideline.
Silently, they eat limestone
and the drifted shells of dead limpets.
They digest the rock in their soft innards,
to build coats of brown spines
and splendid, symmetrical carapaces
which the sea will occasionally
deliver to us intact —
sunbleached, rosy sea-lanterns.

THE FERTILE ROCK
for Áine

In May evening light
an exhausted silver ocean collapses.
It has carried so much to this island,
blue rope and teak beams,
dolphin skulls and fish boxes,
and, once, a metal tank on wheels,
containing one cold passenger.

It rises and collapses at the rim
rises and collapses again —
a mile of white, salt lace
which races across the low limestone terraces,
invades every crack and crevice
in the brown, brine-bitten stone,
and sprays up over
a small grey plateau,
whose fissures brim
with sea pinks.

LADY GREGORY AT CILL GHOBNAIT
for Sheila O'Donnellan

'It was Saint Goban built that church...
she was a king's daughter
and could have married rich nobles...'
Lady Gregory's diary, May 1898

A tiny roofless room —
the rounded window-slit looks past
O Brien's castle to the rising sun —
outside, a granite quernstone
and two bishops' tombs,
a ruined beehive hut
and a tethered, grazing ass.

The patroness of beekeepers had fled
from her people, west across the sea from Clare,
unlike Augusta, who was rowed
across the Gregory Sound from Inishmore,
caught here five days in an October storm,
her son gone off to school,
her husband dead.

Years later, she returned in May, was handed down
from the steamer onto the currach's seat
and sat on the strand to watch three men
hold one end of a net on shore
as, with the other end, three rowed out
to draw half a circle on the lit green sea.

And maybe one of the bantering men
was Peter Coneeley, who had lost his father in a storm,
off the same strand, swept away with two more,
at the end of a human chain,
leaving this sloping field with its church
in the care of his widow and twelve-year-old son.

But on the day that Augusta walked west here,
and sketched the lintel and the leaning jambs,
Gobnait's bees hung, as today,
among bedstraw and whitethorn
and bright young grass.
Only five hundred miles to Euston
and to London's humming dinner tables, calling cards,
yet half of Europe's history lay between
Cill Ghobnait and St James's Park.

Sometimes two cultures are so opposed
through narratives of conquest and control,
that one sees nothing but the other's hackled back,
no shard of beauty, only cruelty and lack.
Sometimes, then, against the odds,
like a voyager alighting from a limestone boat,
someone is drawn to listen, then to act.
For myth and metamorphosis are allied,
shifting how we apprehend the world,
and imperium is dismantled in minds and hearts
or not at all.

Thirteen hundred years had passed
Since Gobnait left Cill Ghrá an Domhain
and travelled on from Inis Óirr,
told in a vision she would find her resurrection and her work
in the place where she came on nine white deer.
Somewhere between Gort workhouse and the House of Lords,
Augusta planted trees,
raised a stone at Raftery's grave,
turned her widow's loneliness to wealth and,
in good faith, did her best to find and mind
the best in both the worlds she spanned.

NAUSTS

There are emptinesses which hold

the leveret's form in spring grass;
the tern's hasty nest in the shore pebbles;
nausts in a silvery island inlet.

Boat-shaped absences,
they slope to seaward,
parallel as potato drills,
curved a little for access —

a mooring stone, fore and aft,
and a flat stone high up,
to guide the tarred bow
of a hooker, *púcán,* or punt

when the high tide lifted it
up and in, then ebbed,
leaving it tilted to one side,
in its shingly nest.

ELIZA MURPHY

What will survive of us is love.
Philip Larkin

Seventeen-month-old Eliza Murphy died
in eighteen twenty-seven
and was buried in April,
in a field south of a garden.

Perhaps spring gales prevented them
from rowing her body
across the short stretch of water
to blessed ground in Killeenaran.

We do not know what brought on her death —
fever, famine or whooping cough.
We do not know whether her hair was black,
or whether her eyes were brown.

We do not know who raised
the carved stone to her memory —
perhaps an older sister or brother, who, later,
sent money from America,

or whether, at low spring tide, she had ever
been carried across the sandbar to the mainland,
past regiments of squirting razor-fish
and sponges like staring moon-cabbages.

Neither can we be sure that she lived
in the row of cottages beyond the garden
or that she was born in one of the rooms
now brimming with sycamores.

We cannot be certain that she had learned
to balance on her feet before illness came
or was able to toddle about on the cobbles.
We cannot know her small store of words.

We know only that she sleeps
where the otter and the fox pad through the long grass
and that she died in April,
dearly beloved.

CRATER

A high corner of the apple tree shakes
as a thrush pecks and pecks at one of the last apples.
The sun slants onto the thrush and the apple
which has a crater in it.

This is what apples are for,
to be turned into song.

The magician I met in Leap Castle
told me that she had grown up
in a magicians' supplies shop in London.
Her father, a seventeen-year-old from Mayo,
his lungs eaten by tuberculosis,
had been nursed by her mother,
a young Londoner,
who, one Monday morning,
brought him a gift,
a book of magic tricks.

All his long months in the sanatorium he practised,
eventually honing tricks which only he could perform.
He could produce from the healed cavities of his chest
seventeen billiard balls,
and who knows how many handkerchiefs,
how many white, fluttering doves.

IN THE UNDERGROUND CAR PARK
for Mary Armstrong

You noticed them first
as we walked back, lost in talk,
through that ill-lit bunker
glimmering with cars.

They drifted like dry pink snow,
blotting bumpers and bonnets,
catching in the iron patterning
of a round man-hole cover.

We drove around the pillars
of the dim underworld
and saw where they billowed
through the metal grilles,

then settled in a deep pink drift
on the grey concrete floor.
You ran and scooped handful
after handful into a summer hat.

The blossom was softer, finer
than anything we could remember -
like music drifted down to Hades
with a promise of cherries.

Two long-haired young men yank at one another's beards;
two fat cats eyeball each other;
two mice tug at an altar-bread held between them,
as though wildness itself yearned for balance.

Oak galls were ground for brown ink;
green woad leaves boiled for blue;
the fur of the marten-cat
bound into a brush;
gold tapped,
finer than fish-skin.

The deft, sharp-eyed young men,
in scriptoria at Kells,
Iona or Lindisfarne,
who bent over work so intricate,
only young eyes could see it
in all its ludic tangle,
may not have been unlike
Traveller boys I taught
who would rather have been charging
in a sulky down an East Galway road in March
or out in night-time fields, lamping rabbits,
than sitting, hunched over a desk,
ears cocked for the returning school bus.

When troubled, they too were calmed
by the rhythm of lighting up a page
with crimson and indigo pens;
their minds were soothed
by stories of terrible trials,
of survival and triumphant good,
involving lions, eagles, gods and men.

LOCH
  for Francis Harvey

To the side of a mountain gap,
light fills the scraped bowl
of high loch Ochóige.
This lake is a secret to which
you can skid down, hazardously,
over a slope of quartzite scree,
or climb up from one of two valleys.
It is a minted silver coin;
a treasure dug out by glaciers;
it is a secret in which to swim,
its water cold, brown, a little bitter —
at each stroke you will tip a little water
over the lake's rough lip.

It gathers the mountains about it
and, as the sun moves around
the mountains are great shutters
like the shutters in Dutch paintings
which slant light onto a jug or a letter
or a lady's yellow cloak,
but here, light is slanted
onto an emptiness
which brims over,
which is replenished.

'WE ARE WHAT WE EAT'

That's what she said,
'Every seven years
almost every cell in our body is replaced.'
I thought of her own art,
how faithfully she rendered
the miraculous lines, the miraculous lives,
of feather and bone —

and I remembered an oak rib,
honeycombed with shipworm,
given as a keepsake to another friend,
who had sailed from Dublin to the Faroes
in a wooden fishing hooker,
which was later rebuilt.

These boats are rebuilt, renamed,
until every plank and rib
has been replaced so often
that nothing remains
except the boat's original lines
and a piece of silver,
hidden under the mast.

ALMA,

I woke up saying the word,
just as, a few mornings earlier, I had woken up
saying 'The Silk Road'.
'Who conducts the music of our dreams?
leaving us with only one clear note — a word for 'soul'
or a name for the most sensuous, the most tortured of early roads,
a name given at a distance, in hindsight,
by someone who had never travelled it —'
not even one clear road either, but several,
a web of camel routes through thorn and sand and storm,
mule tracks over frozen mountain gaps
to where silk worms chewed on mulberry leaves,
spun from their bodies the strong filaments of dreams.

I THOUGHT

only love could do it,
give us moments so complete
there is nothing behind us or before —
only the timbre of that particular voice,
the brush of skin on that particular skin,
soul brushing against that other soul —
but, sometimes, light can do it too,
as it fills every fresh leaf on an April tree,
brightens one side of every limb and twig,
reveals how every one of them was pulled low
by last year's burden
and half the branches pruned and burnt,
how the tip of every down-turned branch, every one,
is upturned now, pink budding through the green —
like the painted, upturned fingers
of temple dancers.

TWO DOORS

There are two entrances to this house
the old priest told us this morning
as he turned, bright as a bird,
to the great oak door under the rose window.
Through one door the people come in,
through the other door the light comes in
and the people are in the light
and the light is in the people.

Few could have wished it otherwise
yet, in the cathedral's thousand years,
so much else has come in the lower door,
borne often by princes of church and state,
while, through the rose window,
through thick dust, through spiders' webs,
with their hoards of netted flies,
the light still enters, limpid, constant.

Coimbra, Portugal, 2010

GREEN CITIES
for Brídín

Coming around a corner today at Rue Fouroy
The scent of newly clipped boxwood is
the scent of Dublin forty years ago,
the scent of summer cities —
a scatter of boxwood clippings on canvas.

Behind the double, upside-down u's
of the green iron stile
white butterflies,
and a man in worn corduroys.
His long-handled clippers click
the child-sized hedges into neat green blocks
opening onto a world of fountains spilling and spilling
their profligate freshness into the summer light.
Round flowerbeds,
musty with lupins, heavy with bees.

And the swings —
oak seats worn to satin,
with iron chains
creaking and creaking solemnly,
weight swinging us up,
in our short-sleeved frocks,
higher and higher,
into the fruiting chestnut trees.

SWANS AT NIMMO'S PIER

They are angels at their morning ablutions
more industrious by far, more hygienic,
more conscientious, than mortals.

More than a hundred oil and rummage their feathers,
nibble themselves vigorously under stomachs and wingpits,
littering the shingle with white quills and breast down.

But in the middle of this white fury
some sleep on, long creamy necks coiled on their backs,
heads folded under their own glorious wings.

Most of these doze on the concrete slip
but a few sleep standing up,
meringues balanced on grey feet.

These dozers are Luciferian swans who,
heads hidden under unnibbled wings,
think darkly, 'I will not scrub.'

Or perhaps they are less resolute,
muttering in their angelic slumbers,
'O Lord, let my wings be well-oiled,
let me be louse-free — but not just yet.'

THE WASHING

April light drenches the washing —
white sheets and pillowcases,
pink towels, blue jeans;
four more bean plants have shoved
their heads up through the horse manure;
green flames flicker
through the tarnished armour
of the apple tree's branches
and, from a breezy, budded twig,
a robin tells the cat that he, the robin,
owns the world.

Inside, on the windowsill,
the sun washes across a photo of my mother,
gentle and pretty in her furred degree gown.
My young father in another photo
poses by a pine tree with his fiddle.
The photos were taken,
long before they met
on two other light-drenched,
given days.

The railway embankment to our left
drives a green line through scree and grizzled heather.
A ghost track carries a ghost train
west from Letterkenny to Burtonport.
On one of the slatted wooden seats
sits a serious fourteen-year-old from Tyrone
with fine, straight, reddish hair.
The train huffs and clanks over our heads
across tall, cut-stone pylons
which flank the narrowest part of the road.

She is travelling to Irish college in Ranafast
in nineteen twenty-nine.
The narrow-gauge train steams along so slowly
that she can reach out
and pull leaves off the occasional, passing tree.
Her friend holds her hat out of the window
and swizzles and swizzles it around, absent-mindedly,
until it spins off and lands amid the scree.

My mother does not know that the railway line was built
by men who believed that the train was foreseen
in the prophecies of Colmcille
as a black pig snorting through the gap.
She cannot prophesy, so she does not know
that her father will be dead within three years,
or that she will meet her husband
and will spend her adult life
west of these rounded, granite hills,

or that, in seventy-five years' time,
one of her daughters will drive her
under this disappeared bridge
and out of Donegal
for the last time.
All she knows is that she is going to Ranafast
and that the train is travelling very slowly.

HALLOWEEN WINDFALLS

These mornings I gather the perfectly sweet apples
which grew too high to pick,
which come down every night in the storm.

They crack and bruise easily
as they strike the grass.

Apples can't swivel on their twigs to catch the sun —
these are all half-red, half-green.

Blackbirds, tits, thrushes,
even crows have dug out their claims.

I wash off the dirt and the sticky leaves,
cut out the damaged bits,
set some sound, delicious ones aside.

I dry these and put some into a paper bag
to bring to my mother in the nursing home.

She used to set aside
the central leaves of the lettuce,
mash the heart of the cabbage
with a little butter and salt,
for the youngest.

DEATH,

the breath heavy and short —
a labour, mucky as birth.

My mother, at almost ninety,
must run a marathon.

Three weeks ago,
she made her last pithy retort;
three days ago, she ate a sliced strawberry;
today she cannot drink a sip —
we have pink sponges on sticks to wet her lips.

We, her greying brood, have arrived
in cars, by train, by plane.
Her room is full of stifled mobile phones.

Death's is a private country,
like love's.

THE RED TREE

The red tree is a giver —
all day long it gives away its leaves,
one or two at a time.
When a dry leaf tumbles down through dry leaves
it sounds like the first drops of heavy rain.

In the evening
when all the last light comes to roost,
the red tree is a lamp
leading us into the dark.

HEDGEHOG

It snuffles across the lawn at night,
a small, silver, trundling boar
with a long nose.

We are seldom quiet enough
to allow the moon to find
with whom we share our ground.

RNA
for Harry Harvey

Last night, on Easter Sunday
my nephew told me
that messenger ribonucleic acids have the task
of translating DNA into protein,
that they carry a cell's blueprint
to be made into fibre and flesh and bone.

This morning I woke up early
but lay on.
My sister's garden was already wide awake.
Above all the chirping and whirring
the blackbird's courting note
rang out — a round gold coin.

Astonishing,
astonishing to know
that the throat muscles, the voice box
and the levitating architecture
of hollow feather and hollow bone,
were coded in the blackbird's DNA,
translated by messenger ribonucleic acids,
were made flesh,
this particular scrap of singing flesh,
which made this particular mating song.

CONSIDER THE COCOSPHERE
for Tim and Mairéad Robinson

Which you will never see
not because it lives in the ocean
but because it is so tiny
that light is too crude a medium
to relay to us
the absurdly beautiful structure
of the plate armour
which this alga creates for itself.

Paired porcelain cartwheels
interlock to form the sphere
which encloses this minute life form.
It drifts around,
just under the skin of the sea,
in blooms so large
they may be seen from space.

You will never see either the cocosphere
or the cocolithophore which it protects —
electrons are needed
to divine the form
of each individual design —
a beauty gratuitous,
as the upper, outer roofs
of cathedrals or mosques,
painstakingly decorated
for the eyes of steeplejacks
and of gods.

BLUE SAXOPHONES

In Buenos Aires the sidewalks are broken,
but the trees are tall and blue,
blue like Cezanne's blue pitcher,
which speaks to some still corner of the soul —
a quite unnecessary, delicate blue —
and the unmended pavements are strewn
with a carpet of blue blossoms,
and with the bent pennies,
the tough leathery purses,
which are the seed cases of the jacaranda —
a surety, until now,
that there would certainly
be more and more of this,
more tall blue trees in October,
singing, gratuitously,
above the dusty pavements
out of thousands of blue
clustered saxophones.

THE IMPORTANT DEAD
for Sabine

In the long stone ship
of St Francis's Abbey
at Ross Errily,
in April evening light,
we decipher the names
of dead, defeated
chieftains, earls, burghers
whose bones were carried here
as Macbeth's were borne off to Iona
or other important dead were borne
to this great abbey or that.

Here, Kirwans, De Burgos, O Flahertys —
Old English, Mere Irish,
an occasional Cromwellian,
who lived in enmity,
amity or uneasy detente,
whose quarrels persist, vaguely,
only in our heads,
now rest, head to toe,
as the wind from the Black River
sifts over their sunken,
their stone-boxed, bones.

Near the bell tower,
our friend has been searching
for owl pellets — gluts of fur,
regurgitated by the soft-winged predators.
She dismantles them in her cupped hand.
As a gust scatters fragments of small skulls
she rescues the jawbone of a field mouse,
and the smaller jawbone of a bank vole,
a very recent invader.

IN THE LAVA PIPE

None of the images of our fissured, creaking earth,
its armour-plating overlapping and melting,
prepared me for life in the sloped tunnel
on a volcano's shoulder,
where a molten current once ran
under the cooling crust.

This is no longer a vision of red hell
but the land of shades itself
This is life turned down
to its lowest register.
If we stand silent in the dark
we hear the soft wingbeats of a bat;
if our ears were keener we might hear
the wingbeats of the tiny insects
whose paths criss-cross in our torch-beams.

The curved walls are clothed in long roots.
They reach down for oxygen, a little moisture
and nutrients from bat-droppings.
Above us, certain flowering trees
grow along the route of the lava pipe,
their lives made possible
by this subterranean nourishment.

We reach the chamber at a rock fall
then turn our torch beams
and make our way back up,
hurrying as much as darkness,
broken rock and roots allow.
Rounding a curve, we see the bright oval
of the cave mouth,

This must be the path which Orpheus took,
his faith failing here, near the cave mouth,
his young beloved turning back
to the dank land of roots.

As he emerged weeping
the animals still understood his music
but, to his bright treble,
there was now added a deep bass
as he stumbled down the mountainside
following a line
of flowering trees.

THE WHITE CYCLAMEN

has flung its five petals back
off its face and furled them
into a light-filled spiral.

It has done this because
it lives under a hazel
and needs to fight for light
and for the attention of bees
whose industry
in the service of sweetness
involves much casual sex
on the part of apple trees
and thistles and cyclamen.

We know that the dust
carried about on the thighs
of the world's bees
still sustains life
on our green and clamorous planet.
The mystery is why, despite
the imperatives of tooth and claw,
the tiny cyclamen's struggle
to propel itself out the soil
autumn after autumn,
millennium after millennium
should result in such grace.

FLOWERS AT LOUGHCREW

How with this rage shall heauty hold a plea
Whose action is no stronger than a flower?
William Shakespeare

We have no key with which to enter
this chamber of the dead
so must peer through an iron gate
along the stone passage
to where a rising sun at equinox
will flash its torch
on flowers and suns —
a seeding and reaping calendar —
like suns and flowers
in a child's copybook.

A friend tells me
that fossil pollen is found
in the earliest burials.
He says this is what makes us human
as much as stone tools —
our ceremony of grief,
attended by what is most beautiful,
most fragrant on this earth.

Today is the last day of our winter.
Ice lingers under the stone lintel
but a brilliant sun reaches far
into the passage,
lights a corner of the backstone faintly,
gives us one carved flower,
picked out in white.

A family plays among the ruined cairns.
The father photographs them,
then gathers them to go
calling on the youngest,
to come along —
'Bríd, Bríd.'

Tomorrow is St Bridget's Day.
We drive home through soft pastureland.
In a low corner of a field
grow patches of greening rushes
and, near an old farmhouse,
on a slope,
strong clumps of snowdrops.

APPLES AND FIRE

As we entered
the dark winter room
there, shining on the table
were apples, gathered
in haste last September —
each one a small lamp.

Later, as the stove's fire
carved into the cold
I began to understand
why fire was worshipped.

To share heat in winter
sweetness in winter,
is to know blessing.

HARMONIC VASES

In the choir of the Collégiale Saint Martin,
just beneath the light-blasted gothic vaults,
are a number of small holes,
the openings of large ceramic pots
placed in the walls
to improve the acoustic.

Lucius Mummius, who destroyed
the theatre at Corinth,
transported its resonating
bronze vessels to Rome
and dedicated them
at the temple of Luna.

In cottages in County Clare,
an iron pot
was buried under the hearthstone
to give resonance to a dancer's step,
to contain the necessary emptiness

for though we wish to live
utterly alive, within our skins,
there lives in us another yearning —
that whatever harmonic is awakened in us
reverberate outwards,
through our voice, our step,
and outwards
and outwards.

at the fragrant honeysuckle
which I have gathered for him,
at the whirled, long, white and yellow petals,
at the long stamens,
which are grace itself
against that utter green.

He counts the furled and fretted blossoms;
notes how they are organised along the stem
in paired groups of two;
marvels at the mathematical regularity
of flowers —
that they should each be accorded
a precise number of petals,
that a code determining this
should be hidden
in something a millionth
of the size of a pinhead.

The doors
of perception
are multifarious.

MIDDAY AT STOCKHOLM AIRPORT

My flight delayed,
I wander into the Kapell beneath the escalator -
a dozen chairs, seats covered in light blue cloth,
a table,
beside it a small, red, unplugged wall-lamp
and an abstract tapestry —
sky, mountains, orange blobs which might be copper mines,
white lines in the foreground which might be cities.

Behind the door are a tiny sink
and a bookshelf. I read the titles —
Bibeln, Psalmboken, Siddur,
Koranens Budskap, Novum Testamentum Graece,
Agatha Christie's *Herkules Nya Storverk,*
below them red and blue prayer rugs, paper towels.

I light two candles
on a stylised Viking ship candelabra
although I know
that in some corner of the world,
men and women are being tortured
in the name of one or other
of the quiet books on the shelf,
I consider laying out the books on the table,
side by side in this peaceable city —

a man rushes in,
pulls out a mat,
pulls off his shoes,
washes his feet,
dries them with a paper towel
kneels down, his joints cracking,
touches the ground three times with his forehead,
repeats something three times,
rolls up the mat, puts on his shoes
and is gone.

All this was meant to be gone long ago,
votive lamps, lighting candles,
bowing towards some holy centre of the earth,
yet sometimes we have to
gather up the four corners of our lives,
like the corners of a tablecloth,
to shake out the crumbs;
sometimes we need light
for a journey,
sometimes we even need to bow.

NIGHT ROAD IN THE MOUNTAINS
for the Berlin String Quintet

The great black hulks of the Bauges
rise so high
that, this midnight,
the plough's starry coulter
is sunk in them.

Earlier, in the small, crowded church,
in the upper valley,
five musicians played for us,
stood, bowed, then played on and on
munificent as a mountain cascade in spring.

We do not know,
we do not understand
how five bows,
drawn across five sets of strings
by gifted, joyful hands, can trace
the back roads of our hearts,
which are rutted
with doubts and yearnings,
which are unpredictable
as this ever-swerving
mountain road
down which we now drive,
hugging the camber,

informed by rhythm
and cadence,
happy to live
between folded rock and stars.

V

KEATS LIVES

(2015)

WINTER VIEW FROM BINN BHRIOCÁIN

In the mountain-top stillness
the bog is heather-crusted iron.
A high, hidden mountain pond
is frozen into zinc riffles.

We have tramped across a plateau
of frost-smashed quartzite
to the summit cairn.

Far below, in February light,
lakes, bogs, sea-inlets,
the myriad lives being lived in them,
lives of humans and of trout,
of stonechats and sea-sedges
fan out, a palette of hammered silver,
grey and silver.

TWO IVORY SWANS

fly across a display case
as they flew across Siberian tundra
twenty thousand years ago,
heralding thaw on an inland sea —
their wings, their necks, stretched,
vulnerable, magnificent.

Their whooping set off a harmonic
in someone who looked up,
registered the image
of the journeying birds
and, with a hunter-gatherer's hand,
carved tiny white likenesses
from the tip of the tusk
of the great land-mammal,
wore them for a while,
traded or gifted them
before they were dropped
down time's echoing chute,
to emerge, strong-winged,
whooping,
to fly across our time.

(British Museum, April 2013)

FINGER-FLUTING IN MOON-MILK

We are told that usually, not always,
a woman's index-finger
is longer than her ring-finger,
that, in men, it is usually the opposite,
that the moon-milk in this cave
retains the finger prints and flutings
of over forty children, women and men
who lived in the late Palaeolithic.
Here, in the river-polished Dordogne,
as the last ice-sheets started to retreat
northwards from the Pyrenees,
in a cave which is painted
with long files of mammoths
and gentle-faced horses,
a woman, it seems, with a baby on her hip
trailed her fingers down through
the soft, white substance
extruded by limestone cave-walls
and the child copied her.
Today, the finger-flutings remain clear,
the moon-milk remains soft;
as we trundle through the cave's maze
in our open-topped toy train
we are forbidden to touch it.

With no gauge to measure sensibility
we cannot know what portion
of our humanity we share
with someone who showed a child
how to sign itself in moon-milk
one day, late in the Old Stone Age.

(Rouffignac, 2010)

were sieved out of the mud of the riverbank
in the cloister of the convent of Santa Clara-a-Vehla,
were dug out of silt with the convent itself
which had started to sink into Mondego waters
one year after the last stone carver had wiped the dust
off the twined leaves, off the doves
above the door capitals.

In May light, broad sandstone vaults
are sand-blasted, clean as stones fallen
from glacial till at the sea's edge —
clean of mud, of candle smoke,
almost of history.

For seven hundred years the waters rose,
drowning the blue-tiled fountain and the cloister gardens.
The nuns raised and raised the church floor
until psalms were sung high among the vaults.
Finally, they built on higher ground.
Farm horses were stabled in the nave,
the rose window became a farmhouse door.

Four battered silver thimbles
were dredged up with needles, scissors,
broken crockery,
cloister tiles.

Crossed lovers,
widowed noblewomen
or peasant girls who placed them
on middle or ring fingers,
who bent their heads
to stitch plain habits or fine altar linen
were sisters, but only
as stars are sisters,
who form a constellation
but inhabit different planes and aeons.
Their stitching talk was
of treachery and love betrayed,
clanking crusades, inquisitions, dynasties.
on the rise or on the wane,
new worlds to the west
full of gold and murder.
They talked of fresh bread, olives
and always the rising waters.

Small things survive inundations —
thimbles,
blue tiles,
doves.

(Coimbra, 2013)

'BEWARE OF THE DOG'

Cave Canem,
the threshold mosaic warned
but not *Cave Montem*;
although there had been earthquakes,
no one suspected the mountain,
or understood the shunt and dive
of the earth's plates
or the burning tides that drive them.

With a long wooden spatula
Celer, the baker, the slave
of Quintus Granius Verus,
slid this round wholemeal loaf,
with both of their names
branded into it,
from the brick oven
hours or minutes before
ash fell like hot snow
and hid their city.

(British Museum, 2013)

BURIAL, ARDÈCHE 20,000 BC

No bear or lion ever raked him up,
the five-year-old child,
victim of illness, accident or sacrifice,
buried in a cave floor
high above a white-walled, roaring gorge
shortly after the ice-sheets had retreated.

Someone sprinkled his grave with red ochre,
someone tied a seashell around his neck,
someone placed a few flint blades by his side,
and under his head someone laid
the dried tail of a fox, perhaps
a white fox.

IN THE TEXTILE MUSEUM
for M. Cannon (1915–2005)

These are the cloths of Egypt:
a baby's silk bonnet,
padded and lined, and trimmed
with strips of faded,
finely-stitched
red and green linen;

a tapestry tunic ornament
with its woven image
of a woman in a short tunic
carrying a baby on her back
across a river;

a fine wool curtain
whose perfect, threadbare
blue, green and orange fish
for seventeen centuries
have flashed to and fro
through its watery weave;

I will never meet the weavers
of Antinöe on the Nile
but I remember the swish and click-click-click
of my mother's treadle sewing machine
as she bent to it, intent;
the tissue rustle of a dress pattern
as she sliced through it

with her good scissors;
her appraising eye, by the sitting-room fire,
as she measured a growing piece of knitting
against the arm of one or other growing child,
while behind her, on a high shelf
her books of poetry,

bought before she married,
sat under light dust.

Love slips easily through the eye of a needle,
words clothe us;
not everything ends up in a book.

(Musée des Tissus, Lyon)

I WANTED TO SHOW MY MOTHER THE MOUNTAINS —

the Bauges in deep snow,
pink in the evening light.
Why did I want to show her mountains
five years after she was dead?
She was as terrified of heights
as any eighteenth-century traveller...
Perhaps I wanted to show her mountains
because so often she had said,
'Oh, look, look!'

BEES UNDER SNOW

In a valley beside the black wood,
this year there are fifty-two beehives —
orange and blue cubes with zinc lids,
raised on long girders.

Last winter, under a foot of snow,
they were square marshmallows in a white field.
By a minuscule door lay a few dead bees
and one or two flew about distractedly
but the bees inside hovered in a great ball
shivering to keep warm, to stay alive,
moving always inwards towards the globe's centre
or outward towards its surface.

As much as their hunt for sweetness
or their incidental work, fertilising the world's
scented, myriad-coloured flowers
to bear fruit for all earthbound, airborne creatures,
this is part of their lives,
these long months of shivering, of bee-faith.

NOVEMBER SNOW

Our boots creak down through a foot
of white shafted with blue. The hedges,
humped and swayed under huge burdens,
are white mammoths' heads.

From under a smothered bush
to the trunk of a young oak,
runs a tiny track,
oval prints on both sides of a broken line —
someone's frozen tail.

and the young oak scatters
wide its bounty —
gold bullion on white linen.

PRIMAVERA

A first sighting,
five low primroses,
and later, near the compost,
a sliver of white among clumped shoots —
a snowdrop splits its green sheath,
and high birdsong in the hazels —
a jolt to realise that here too,
below snow-shawled Alps
with their tunnels and ski-stations,
this is Saint Bridget's Eve.

This is the evening when my father
used to knock three times on the scullery door
and wait for an invitation to enter
with a bundle of cut rushes, saying

'Téigí ar bhur nglúine,
fosclaigí bhur súile
agus ligigí isteach Bríd.' *

Older, he told me his sisters used to vie
to be the one to knock three times
before entering with the first greening.
What ritual were they re-enacting?
Or we, in the warm yellow kitchen, suddenly full
of rushes and scissors and coloured wool-ends,
what ceremony were we weaving there,
folding the silky stalks into crosses
to hang above the door
of each room in the house,
or what do those little island girls celebrate

who still carry the *Brídeóg*, the spring doll,
from house to welcoming house,

if not the joyful return
of the bride of Hades after three months of deep
wintering, if not a first sighting of Persephone
among the rushes in a wet western field?

And what caution was told in the hesitation,
until that third knock granted admission,
what fear of deception, of late frosts,
of February snow and dead lambs?

Our fears are different now,
of floods and fast-calving glaciers,
of birds and beasts and fish and flowers forever lost
and the earth's old bones pressed for oil.

But our bones still bid her welcome
when she knocks three times,
when she enters, ever young,
saying

Kneel down,
open your eyes
and allow spring to come in.

---

* *Téigí ar bhur nglúine, fosclaigí bhur súile agus ligigí isteach Bríd.*
('*Kneel down, / open your eyes / and allow Bridget to come in.*')

THE TUBE-CASE MAKERS

(Les Ephemères)

This one-inch mottled twig
is built of silk and stone.
Inside it, under a larva's translucent skin,
are shadowy, almost-ready wings,
a heart that pumps and pumps.

For two or three years
it trundled about
in the shallows of a mountain river
in this stone coat, eating leaf-debris,
adding, as it grew, a little sticky silk
to one end, a few more tiny stones,
until the time came to shut itself in,
to almost seal both ends of its tube —
as intent on transformation
as any medieval anchorite.

It is not true that it
turns into a green soup
but how does it happen,
the breaking down of redundant muscles,
the building of flight muscles
as a grub becomes stomachless,
rises out of the river,
for one summer's day, to mate,
alight at nightfall,
and lay the eggs
that have kept its tribe alive
since it rose in clouds
around the carbuncled feet of dinosaurs —

with each tiny,
down-drifting egg
encapsuling
a slumbered knowledge
of silk,
stone
and flight?

FLY-CATCHER

Last month, Doris, the bird-bander,
told us about a one-legged bird, a fly-catcher
who traced the spine of the Appalachians
year after year, and flew south,
balancing her tiny, tattered body
down through Mexico
all the way to South America
and back to the same Philadelphia hedgerow
to draw breath among cat-birds and orioles,

to be caught in the same birders' net,
to raise brood after brood, and then
to balance on a twig,
on her single, fettered leg,
to feed on passing insects,
to store fat for her next Odyssey.

Life can be so rough,
yet we can't get enough of it.

KEATS LIVES ON THE AMTRAK
for Jim and Kathy Murphy

Today, on the clunking, hissing, silver train
between Philly and New York,
the African-American conductor squeezed himself
into the dining car seat opposite,
genially excused himself and,
when I responded, asked why my novel
was full of page-markers —
'You have it all broken up' —
and I said that I was teaching it.

He leaned forward, smiled, and said,
'I'm going to get a tee-shirt with
Keats Lives on it. This time of year,' —
he gestured towards the window,
trees were blurring into bud —
'when everything starts coming green again,
I always think of him...
A thing of beauty is a joy forever,
Its loveliness increases, it will never
Pass into nothingness; but still will keep
A bower quiet for us...'
I told him that it was a Dublin taxi-driver
who first told me
that Keats claimed his only certainties were
the holiness of the heart's affections
and the truth of imagination.

He took a ballpoint from
the pocket of his uniform jacket,
wrote down the quote,
asked where it came from,
as I had done, two decades earlier
in the back of a taxi,
as hundreds had
since the young, sick apothecary
penned it to his friend.

'That is a bombshell', he said,
'I'm going to give that to my little girl tonight —
Oh, light-winged dryad...'
The intercom announced *Next stop, Trenton*,
the steel wheels began their long scream.
He hauled himself out of the seat,
smiled again and, drawing a line
across his chest with his thumb, said,
'*Keats Lives*'.

AT THE END OF THE FLIGHT

from Dallas to Philadelphia
the flight attendant announced
that we had the father and sisters
of a fallen soldier on board,
that we were to remain seated
until they disembarked,
that she had died honourably.

There was a round of applause
and another on landing;
a middle-aged man in a beige jacket
stood to take down his hand luggage —
a carrier-bag with the corner
of a folded, starry flag poking out —
and two young women in jeans
rose from separate seats
further down the plane
and we heard the sound of grief
grinding three separate tunnels
through their days.

SNOW DAY

Snow
like manna
fell through the night.
By my closed window
the cypress's fingers
strain under mounds
of white.
Deep deer tracks
pass the front door,
halt at the hedge,
start again, deeper,
at the other side.

Snow fell and fell
through the night,
feeding our need
for silence,
for mid-winter light,
for believing that all can be
cleansed,
made right.

DO THE SUMS

The last of the brown-headed matches
that filled the box so snugly
rattles about on its own;

the tideline wears a fluttering feather boa —
shed, feather by curved feather,
from the breasts of a hundred swans;

the tap, dripping slowly all night,
has filled the basin to brimming;

so why am I astonished
to find myself over fifty,
at least half of my life gone.

SHRINES

You will find them easily,
there are so many —
near roundabouts, by canal locks,
by quaysides —
haphazard, passionate, weathered,
like something a bird might build,
a demented magpie
bringing blue silk flowers,
real red roses,
an iron sunflower,
a Christmas wreath,
wind chimes,
photographs in cellophane,
angels, angels, angels
and hearts, hearts, hearts
and we know
that this is the very place
the police fenced off with tape,
that a church was jammed
with black-clad young people,
that under the flowers and chimes
is a great boulder of shock
with no-one to shoulder it away
to let grief flow and flow
like dense tresses of water
over a weir.

AT KILLEENARAN
for Carol

We stood in a curve of seaweed
in light grey rain
with our jacket hoods up,
watching two seals
that hovered just beyond the tideline.

Their eyes were as calming as those
of a pair of Byzantine saints
gazing at us from an icon screen.

Then we turned about
and saw a sky-high arch,
all seven colours humming,
both ends firmly planted
in the ebbing tide of the estuary
and outside, above it,
in the blustered clouds
a bigger arch, very faint,
but absolutely there.

LAMENT

Let me learn from the Brent geese
their grey grammar of grief
as they wheel in a bow-backed flock
onto a February tide.

Let me learn from these strong geese
to map my losses with a cry,
learn from those who are always losing
a chick, a lover, a brother,
losing one cold country or another.

Let me learn from the black-necked geese
how to bend my shoulders low
over a wrack-draped shore,
let me learn from the curlew's long weep,
Oh, oh, oh, oh, oh.

CLASSIC HAIR DESIGNS

Every day they are dropped off
at Classic Hair Designs,
sometimes in taxis,
sometimes by daughters,
often by middle-aged sons
in sober coats
who pull in tight by the kerb,
stride around to the door
and offer an arm.

How important this
almost last vestige
of our animal pelt is.
How we cherish it —
the Egyptians' braided bob,
those banded Grecian curls,
the elaborate patterns of Africa,
the powdered, teetering pompadour,
the sixties' long shining fall over a guitar,

and the fine halo
of my almost-blind
ninety-two-year-old neighbour,
permed and set
in the style
in which she stepped out
with her young man
after the last World War.

GENIUS

There is a man who polishes the brass handrails
of the curved staircase in the National Library.
He polishes them often, and with great attention.
They shine like the brass kettles that
were polished weekly, on a Tuesday
or a Thursday, then put back like soft lamps
onto the sideboards of old people's homes.
I greet him. He smiles and keeps shining,
rubbing off the drying green polish.

When I borrow books
I sometimes find that the writers
who wanted to dream a nation into being
or forge its conscience
or reveal its hypocrisies, have sat
and read at these same green tables.
They have all walked up the same staircase
holding or leaning on the brass rails
which are brazen serpents,
curved bands of light.

The man who keeps the rails gleaming,
who brushes up the rain-soaked leaves outside,
has written no books.
He is a genius of care,
the genius of the place.

CLEAN TECHNOLOGY

In the spring of '92
the French government,
in consultation with Doctor Antoine Louis,
Secretary of the Academy of Surgery in France,
entrusted the construction of the first guillotine
to Tobias Schmidt, maker
of clavichords and pianofortes.
He proposed a slanted
rather than a rounded blade,
tested the machine on animals
and on human corpses
till it sang.

In the summer of that year,
when he applied for a patent,
the ministry of the interior refused him —

'It is repugnant to humanity
to issue a patent
for an invention of this nature.
We have not yet reached
such an excess of barbarity.'

MOLAISE

Odd that he should be quartered here
where regiments mustered and marched
and orders were barked at straight-backed men.
His gaze has outlasted sword and fire,
the quiet gaze that fell for seven centuries
on the lintel and jambs of his stone house
and — when he was carried out, shoulder high —
on Sliabh League, Ben Bulben and Knocknarea,
on the deep walls and the speckled stones
of Inishmurray, where pilgrims made their stations
hoping to shed their agitation, if not their cares.

What drew me to this stillness
on many damp Dublin Saturdays,
my spirit at seventeen or twenty
a turbulence, a lurching boat?
I knew nothing of stormy Inishmurray,
its monks and poitín-makers,
but was drawn to this oak sculpture
with the cheekbones of an Asian sage.
Sages were almost as suspect as saints
but Molaise was quiet as a Henry Moore
and touched the same ground in me.

And who was the artist carved it
seven centuries after the battle,
fought over a book's copyright,
seven centuries after Colmcille

came to Molaise in remorse
to receive a penance of green martyrdom
which sent him to Iona in the north?

Where did the sculptor learn his art?
And who was the commissioning abbot?
— eager, perhaps, to draw a pilgrim trade
away from Armagh, Derry or Lough Derg —
a businessman maybe, who dealt
in curses and blessings, or maybe not,
for the corrupt middle ages were also the age
of Francis who listened to wolves and birds,
Hildegard who healed and left us songs,
and Julian who tells us 'All shall be well'.

I, now in middle age, am past denying
that I have known women and men
in whose presence I am calmed and blessed,
under whose compassionate gaze I am complete
as the storm-rounded stones on Inishmurray's beach.

WWW.ANNALSOFULSTER.COM

When my O Canannain ancestor
pillaged the sanctuary of Lough Derg
in the eleventh century
and carried off its gold vessels,
he could hardly
have foreseen that letters
put down carefully
by some tonsured scribe
would light up on a screen
a thousand years later.

How could he have
divined the power
of an inked feather,
of the quartz seam
ticking under the heather?

THE SINGING HORSEMAN

The bay horse, with its golden
chest and head, is from another world,
is kin to wide-winged Pegasus,
or to the white horse that carried Oisín off,
or to the black mare of Fanad
who saved her rider from a demon.

But this golden-headed rider is one of us,
a young man with a torn red sleeve
jogging home, bareback, from the races
on a breezy summer's evening in Sligo,
riding near the rough blue shore
heading north towards Streedagh,
playing a whistle or singing,
and the painter, who paints them both,
is an old man who remembers a hundred races,
a hundred summers' evenings.

But how are we, who do not believe
in magic steeds, to understand this,
except to remember the years
between fifteen and twenty-two
when our spirits strained as a moth's
wings strain inside its brown, spun prison,
when a song — pressed into black vinyl

by some Dylan, seeking his direction home,
or sung by an acquaintance at a party,
giving voice to some long dead passion —
released our crumpled spirits,
transported us across skies and oceans
and our hands, our heads,
were golden.

(National Gallery, Dublin)

TREASURE

Yesterday, among green-shouldered reeds,
I found a treasure — no young Moses,
but a water-hen who steered six fistfuls
of black down through a motley of shadows.

Disturbed, she made for her nest,
stamped loudly on its dry reeds
and pecked the slowest on its bald crown
as it grappled its way up.

In an empty nest this morning
the red-gartered cock hauls in dry stalks
to build up a small round Venice;
it sinks daily on its brittle pylons.

A bright-beaked clockwork toy,
he motors upstream to the canal bridge
where his mate guards their long-toed chicks;
they clamber over broken reeds and bottles.

A tiny black frenzy paddles behind the hen
as the parents call them all out into the bright
heat at the edge of the reed-bed.
Only one was lost in the night.

THREE MOUNTAIN GAPS

The crooked gap, high
on the shoulder of Derryclare:
across it, a rapier of pink light.

The V-shaped gap at the end of Gleninagh
through which, at winter solstice,
the sun sets, now a little off-centre,
to brighten an alignment of white stones —
a bog-abandoned calendar.

The glacier-rounded gap beside Loch Ochóige,
where, earlier, as we clambered up the slope,
a heron, soft-winged pterodactyl-shadow,
passed over our heads,
through its upside-down,
triumphal arch.

EAVESDROPPING

Late at low tide, one June evening,
at the tip of a green promontory
that brimmed with lark song and plover cry,
on a slab of damp granite encrusted
with limpets and barnacles, I lay down,
laid my head down in that rough company
and heard whispers
of a million barnacles,
grumbling of a hundred limpets,
and behind them the shushing
of the world's one
gold-struck, mercury sea.

KILCOLMAN

Great force must be the instrument but famine must be the mean, for
till Ireland be famished it cannot be subdued...
A Briefe Note of Ireland

In my palm lie three rabbit bones
picked clean by an owl who carried them home
to this last tower of a castle where a poet
praised his queen in limber verse,
where every bank now brims with primroses
in a spring that is late and most intense.

Here cattle fields are electric-fenced,
mallard and moor-hen nest on the lake
and steps descend to a covered well;
here, the adventurer knew little peace,
gave little in return, but laboured to praise
the power that brought him into this place.

From here his grandson would send to Lord Cromwell,
a plea against banishment to Connacht,
would claim that, having come to the age of discretion,
he had renounced his mother's popish religion,
that in that province he would be placed in peril
as his late grandfather's writings 'touching
on the reduction of the Irish to civility'
had brought upon him 'the odium of that nation'.

How barbarous the price of courtly ways,
The castle torched, a new-born child dead,
the poet dying in London 'for want of bread';
earlier, the slaughter at Smerwick
and in subdued Munster the Irish, starved and sick,
Creeping from their wooded cover on their hands,
for their legs would not carry them.
How hard, even still, to love the well-turned verse,
whose felicities were turned on such a lathe.

ST STEPHEN'S — A SPECULATION

On an April morning two young women
plant a poplar tree in St Stephen's Green.
In a grid of straight streets
the fingernail curve of St Stephen's Street
with a tall hotel at the far end
traces the northern edge
of a lost monastic enclosure; its bell
rang out over a black pool
before Viking ships made landfall at the Long Stone.
The enclosure came to hold St Mary's Abbey
and the leper hospital of St Stephen
which owned a grazing green to the east
through which, many centuries later,
a fictional student of the same name
would stroll out, hands sunk in his pockets
to become almost as real as Hamlet.

He strolled out well after The Liberator's time,
after the hospital had been renamed
and St Mary's Abbey replaced with a soaring nave
under whose altar lie the bones of St Valentine,
a Roman martyr, portrayed with an orchid,
as his feast day replaced the shepherds' spring feast
of Lupercalia — and who knows what ritual site
the lost monastery might have replaced
near the meeting of four great roads,
what shepherding of fertility and death,
what grove of sacred trees
above a black pool.

THE SUM OF THE PARTS

It was partly the collage of regrowth
displayed in front of the small library,
in a city that has suffered greatly —
an image of green tendrils,
softening the oblongs of tall city blocks;
and it was partly the welcome
of scented candles floating in glasses
and the words on a screen beside them,
words carried across oceans and the reefs of language;
and it was partly the graciously-offered cup of wine,
and the grandmother who humoured
a little boy, pretending to bite his hand
as he tugged at her gold earring;
and the young, smiling pair across from them,
and the mentally disabled man
who found it hard to listen but who listened anyway —

but it was mostly the two women who arrived late,
their white canes tapping either side
of the narrow aisle of the library auditorium.
They walked up to the front with their guide
and had space made for them in the first row
and afterwards asked us to write our names in ink
beside raised Braille,
which left us humbled, honoured
to be servants of the word.

                    (Biblioteca Fernando Gómez Martinez,
                            Medellín, Colombia)

THE HANG-GLIDERS
for Jean O'Donnell and Nico Bernier

This afternoon we saw them,
huge rainbow-coloured butterflies
high above us as we swam in the lake —
so many sons of Daedalus
who, in search of that ever-longed-for lightness,
run and jump off a cliff,
steer themselves about for hours in the air,
skim mountain ridges,
levitate on thermals
and, almost always,
avoid assumption into storm clouds.

Later we pass them, two-legged mortals
in shorts and t-shirts
who solemnly lay out their sails in the shade.
They fold and pack with exquisite care
each cord, each of the pleats
on which their lives depend, in order.

I recall the huge butterflies
I saw in the botanic gardens
emerging from their upside-down capsules,
first the head, then the strong legs
pressing against the papery cockpit lid,
and then, tumbling out slowly,
those exquisitely crumpled wings.

ACOUSTICS

Those tall medieval cathedrals
were set as nets for light,
built as sound-boxes
for psalms, for praising choirs.

When I open my back window wide
it is clear that my small room
was built to tremble with the tune
of a treetop blackbird in June.

THE GREENING

The mountains, the built-up valley,
drink the sky.

After a full night of summer thunder
rattling from one end of the sky to the other,
of lightning and rain battering
the hard, cinnamon-coloured earth,
everything dreeps green again.

Clouds hunker among the summits
of lower mountains
and the high Alps are hidden.

Grass stands up again in the garden
as tree-furred mountainsides drink up,
bringing the sky's dark
into every leaf tip,

and already
under bare summits
gentians have turned thunder
into blue velvet.

ANTRIM CONVERSATION

Pain and suffering are a kind of false currency passed from hand to hand until they meet someone who receives them but does not pass them on.
Simone Weil

Chalk is stained brown near the waterfall.
It crumbles away easily
as flint nodules are prised free;
the flint itself is poised
to split into slivers,
a suggestion of blades,
a memory of the trade
this sharp wealth engendered.

The small, tidy man who paused on his stick
to talk to us in the lane,
on this Sunday of rose-hips and blackberries,
had a voice soft as chalk.
He spoke first of weather and houses and sheep,
of a life working 'to put wee shoes on wee feet'
and we talked on and on in September sunshine
until nodules of hurt washed out
in the stream of his words.

He spoke of being shaken awake as a child
by uniformed men with guns;
of his own young son beaten up;
of prison, of 'not knuckling under',
and then of his satisfaction on hearing
a man's head had been blown off
in a neighbouring town.

History's hard cart rattled on
as flint nodules shattered
into narrow weapons.
We wondered, dumb,
what shift of bedrock,
what metamorphosis,
might heal such wounded,
wounding ground.

What do we know of the chalk,
the flint, of others' souls
or of our own
or of what might break in us,
if history's weight
pressed heavily down?

How do we know
that we could hold the pain
and not pass on
the false and brutal coin?

MOMENT

Within our sliver of the earth's time, was his
a moment in the evolution of our blue globe
akin to that moment when a tiny
multi-legged creature dared to live out of water?
A man who kept repeating, 'forgive, forgive,
be not afraid, be not afraid', a man
who had a god for a parent, as had Achilles,
but no god-given armour.

Did his death mark the end of the heroic age,
or had the age of heroes already waned
as Homer forged his song of ships
and valour and flame-wrapped Troy
and Hector hauled behind a chariot?
Did that blind man set Priam's love in balance
forever, with Achilles's strength and pride?

Hadn't Siddhartha already ridden out
and seen and felt and taken to himself
the wretchedness of all the earth?
and weren't there others before them
struck by some inner or outer light
whose compass was compassion and love?

Was this his triumph, to say it again,
in all those parables to say it again and again
and, knowing the red trough that awaited him,
to put back that struck-off ear,
to bless, not the victorious and the strong,
but the peacemakers, the meek?

GALANTHUS

Head down
spring's small white herald
gallant in green stripes and chevrons
braves the mud and gales
of January.

VIEWING THE ALMOND BLOSSOM

This was an exercise the Japanese poets
repeated every year
as though some lessons could not be
well enough learnt —

how a brown twig puts out
small pugilists' fists
which open, fragrant burst
after fragrant burst
right to the stem's tip.

THE COLLAR

In the corner of the vast, captured mosque
of Abd al-Rahman —
a spreading forest
of salvaged Roman pillars, Arab arches,
and a cathedral like a perched stork —
in the cordial city, where for a time
Muslims, Christians and Jews lived
and worked in amity,
above the locked iron gates of a chapel
dedicated to the Virgin Mary,
we saw a small, dusty medallion
containing a castellated coat of arms,
the inscription *Ave Maria, Gratia Plena,*
and a turbaned moor
chained in an iron collar.

And the mosque
began to fill
with the clatter of crusades,
aroma of the baked crescents of Vienna,
stink of the mass graves of Srebrenica,
the dust of the toppled towers of New York,
hum of drones over Pakistan,
the clank of that collar-chain
and weeping of those who were chained
and who chain in turn —

many victories,
many collars,
little grace.

(Córdoba, 2013)

233

ALICE LICHT

Three ordinary shoe brushes in a museum case,
the kind of brushes whose soft swish
I used hear every morning —
my father 'feeding the leather'
of his creased brown shoes.

'The Reich needs brushes', the half-blind
Otto Weidt insisted, thumping the table
of a Berlin police station
'and I need my Jews to make them.
Give me back my Jews'.

With the help of his ally,
the policeman,
he got them back —
those blind and deaf Jews
and some he pretended were blind and deaf.
He led them back in a long line
like children holding hands,
children released
from a door in the mountainside,
to Rosenthaler St.,
where they worked for two more years
making brushes, binding brooms,
in his small factory in the *Höfe*
with its narrow rooms
painted with pink and green borders,
with its windowless room at the end
where he hid a Jewish family.

And once he drove in his car
to the gates of Auschwitz 'to sell brushes' —
as if any brush could clean a hell-floor —
his purpose being to carry back
three Jews, a young woman — Alice Licht —
and her parents.

The parents died
as did, in the end,
all the blind and deaf brush-makers,
in spite of Otto's ruses and bribes.
They were swept up one morning
late in the war,
by men in shining boots.

His message
was passed to Alice Licht
and she, at last,
escaped to Berlin,
stood at his window
as the war ended,
a small light,
like courage
or blind hope.

BILBERRY BLOSSOM ON SEEFIN
for J.

Halfway between mist and cloud,
we saw it by the barbed-wire fence —
pink-edged boxwood,
and the flowers, rosy cats' bells,
so round and waxy we took them for berries
but May is too early.
And after that there were low clumps everywhere,
the tiny bells secretive as nipples.
It bloomed through last year's heather
up near the summit,
where we unwrapped our sandwiches
as wind sheared through an empty tomb

and I imagined the bilberry-pickers
who used to climb the hills in August,
long-dead boys and girls —
cattle-herders, butter-makers,
singers, dancers — brash and shy
as any disco- or club-goer
and full of the tug of summer's long desire.

And on our way down, just across the path
from a storm-flayed swatch of pine
grew great clumps of the pink and green bushes.
And later still
as we drove down the mountain road
they grew tall along the verge,
so we pulled in and picked big bunches

to carry home
all the ringing promise
of that blossom and leaf
we had often seen before
but had never heard.

VI

DONEGAL TARANTELLA

(2019)

ISLAND CORRIE

Curving back by the northern cliffs,
where a pale scar shows
that another slice of mountain
has succumbed
to this century's
hard seas
and grey storms,
we halt at a rim,
and, far below us,
in June sunlight,
blows the big, elongated O
of Lough Bunnafreva,
ringed, in this summer's long drought,
with a necklace of bleached schist.

Cupped palm of Croaghaun,
gift of a glacier,
silver doubloon of Achill.

AT THREE CASTLES HEAD WE CATCH OUR BREATH

We come from a hidden ocean and go to an unknown ocean.
Antonio Machado

A flat, faulted slab of cliff soars
and shimmers far above us
then slants far below,
into a young ocean
we call the Atlantic.

Bedded sandstones
have been tilted on edge here —
dust of disappeared mountains,
compressed beneath the weight
of disappeared oceans.

What cosmic accident engendered
this relentless complexity of being —
the hot metal core, the mantle heavily swirling
under new hills, thin-floored oceans, fragile cities,

and under the flowering bank of earth behind us,
which responds again to the nearing of a star,
each unfolding primrose an inch of yellow velvet,
each heavy violet teetering on its slim stem,

and us, latecomers,
balanced between cliff and flowers,
trying to comprehend both,
trying to catch our breath.

FOUR HERDS OF DEER

at the back of Djouce mountain,
blent into the heather, hardly visible —
they stared at us, whistled
and sprang away,
white rumps in the air,
light, light, as deer on cave walls.

FLOWERS KNOW NOTHING OF OUR GRIEF
for Eivlin, Kieran and Patrick

The dog creeps out of her bed at night,
pads towards the bedroom door,
bumps against it as she turns to lie down,
whimpers, stays close
and licks her paw.

But the roses, pink and delicate,
unfurl their buds in the sunshine,
scent the steps up to the front door.

Their indifference should break us,
instead, they shore up a dyke
against despair;
they play a tune in a minor key;
they whisper among themselves
in an old Esperanto;
they intimate
that hope is never dead
until this bewildered earth stops
throwing up roses.

11.06.2016

MAL'TA BOY, 22,000 BC

The palaces of the tsars rise up again
newly gilded and painted, along the Neva.
Curled up in a dusty display case
in a corner of their great palace
is the rickle of a four-year-old child's bones,
found under a stone slab
by a lake in eastern Siberia.
Half of his skull painted red,
he was buried with his necklet and bracelet,
his arrowheads and swan amulet.

Small nomad, buried as your people
moved on their circuits, tracking herds
of reindeer and mammoth,
flocks of waterbirds,

a slice of your arm bone is pored over
by tribes of scientists in laboratories.
On bright screens,
they unravel the hidden
code of your genes,
shoot images around the globe
to track skeins of our human journeys
eastwards and westwards,
across three continents —
footfalls on rock, on snow, on grass
in sandy river fords.

Fallen sparrow,
improbable little kinsman,
buried with a baby sibling,
what are the filaments
that join us?
Did you pull flowers
when the snows melted?
Did you run after flapping birds?
Did you die in affliction
or in your sleep?
What did you call your mother?
For how many moons
did she weep?

THE IDIOT

Yesterday I crossed the Neva,
this morning I climbed the chipped, grubby stone stairs
to Alexander Blok's apartment, where he lived,
first in modest comfort
then, after the revolution,
where he shivered, starved and died.

This afternoon I crossed
a small park behind a street
to the apartment where Anna Akhmatova
moved in with her lover, his wife and daughter,
saw the corridor where her lover set up his darkroom,
where her student son set up home.

Three nights this week we ate
in a restaurant called 'The Idiot'.

Is there any tourist so idiotic
as one who rummages for a writer's soul
in her desk; among all the lame,
rejected, ink-and-paper tigers;
among the photos on the dining-room wall;
among the plates and pots on his kitchen shelf?

Blok's desk is as neat as a managing director's;
a writer's saucepan is only slightly
less shiny than the average,
but for that revealed inner life,
that record of yearning and survival,
which reached an arm out to save us,
in the youthful nights

when black waves crashed in,
one burying the other,
for that, we must go back
and turn page
after tattered page.

EXILE

The Shah of Iran
sent a present of an elephant
to the Tsar of Russia.

He had it delivered to a southern port
from which it was walked north
through villages where it terrified the serfs.

When it arrived in St Petersburg
it sickened, and did not live long,
although it was given vodka.

ONE OF THE MOST FOOLISH QUESTIONS...

I ever asked was of a young
historian in Florida.
I asked her that Irish question,
used to keep conversation flowing,
if she knew where her family
had come from originally.

She paused and said, 'It is difficult —
you can tell a certain amount from
auction sales records and cargo lists.'

But one family, she said, had a song,
which they had managed
to track back
to a village in Senegal.

BREAD

The suitcase is only half-unpacked
the washing not done,
the floor not swept,
but the oven is humming,
a sticky bowl and spoon
are in the sink
and the old alchemy of water,
flour and leaven has begun.

Soon high crusts will gild,
three loaves will be tapped
from their tins,
an aroma will flow
through keyholes,
will slip
over chipped saddle-boards,

proclaiming more eloquently
than a thrush delivering
its blue and gold aria
from the top of a telegraph pole,
than a procession
with lifted banners
and trumpets,
than a dog panting wagging circles
around a room,
Home, home, home, home!

GRAFFITI MAKES NOTHING HAPPEN

The summer before last, four girls
scraped their names in large letters,
ANGEL, CRYSTAL, KERRI + KIMI,
into the old sand cliff at Shanganagh
and beside them wrote LOVE + COMPASSION.

Above them, sand martins
swung and hunted in the moist air,
scribed the sky with nib-quick wings,
then homed into their cliffside burrows,
nurseries to a hundred fledglings.

As the girls wrote,
a milk-blue tide behind them
diligently sifted the shingle, turned
each veined pebble over again,
found it a new resting place.

The girls went home
and the martins flew down to Africa
but the cliff still beams out its blurring message,
to dogs and walkers, and to a roiling
brown, winter sea, which tosses up
rocks and plastic bottles and dead young seals.

SAND MARTINS AT SHANGANAGH
for Kevin and Bridget O Donoghue

The loves and dogged housekeeping of sand martins
undermine cliffs of clay, sand and gravel,
laid down by oceans, great rivers and glaciers.

Their burrows puncture a layer of finest sand.
Blithe sappers, they hardly care that
when they are well south of the equator,
sea gales and weeks of winter rain
might conspire to bring down
chunks of the old sand cliffs

despite the frantic scrambling
of cliff-edge briars to hold on, hold on,
the futile claims of fence posts
which dangle for months from barbed wire
before tumbling from cliff-top to shore,
or the protests of the last fragments
of a railway built to carry day-trippers,
in straw hats and starched frocks,
along a track which now crosses
spaces of the imagination.

The railway's chiselled granite blocks
are long fallen to the shingle,
corners smoothed and rounded
by a century of spring tides.

But the sand martins are indifferent
to railways and forgotten journeys.
Their tasks are old and urgent.
They have chicks to feed,
to school in a geometry of grace;
to train, on newly fledged wings,
to shoot out, up over the golf course
and the glowing buttercup fields
then down over a seaweed-draped shore
darting in twittering ellipses,
unchartable to mathematics,
as they prey on flying insects
then slip into the sandy cliff-face

until, if their frail houses last out the rain,
they have gathered enough fat and are fit,
as summer light shifts down to autumn
to fly south to Africa, to face storms
and droughts our kind may have brought on,
as their wing-feathers, reed-bones,
and ever more mysterious memories
stitch northern and southern hemispheres.

A THREE-SEAL MORNING

Yesterday's storm rearranged the shingle
onto fresh mounds and ridges

but now, the sun has laid a gold finger
on the incoming folds of the sea.

Three seals hang in the water, noses up
near a round of stones and seaweed
which could be the drowned village of Longnon.

A small wave draws its breath in
and oval pebbles at the sea's edge

lean forward, faces at a concert —
a long, clicking stone-ripple —
then, gently, fall back.

AT SHANKILL BEACH

When a wave hauls back
it leaves its gleam in saturated sand
and, sudden, up from below, the lugworms
push the darkened sand in little coils and hills.

Where are they going in the dark,
working their tiny miracle,
turning plants into animals again,
eating their way blindly
through their known world?

WINTER MORNING, THE IRISH SEA

This sea has been described as snotgreen,
but, this morning, it is dishwater grey.
Waves slant in from the north,
rear up and collapse on themselves,
retreat in a rattle of sea-stones.
I think no one could love it
as the indigo Atlantic is loved

but I turn south and the sun,
a quick green dot, a red blip
starts up, flings a gold arm out across
the bay, a god of morning yawning,
and then the whole burning lid
is sitting up on the world's rim
and the sea is shaken silver silk
and white lace froths in and in and in
along the whole stony length of the shore.

RETURNS

I

May the second, and the sand martins are back with the sun.
Was there ever such excitement at a home-coming
as they dive in and out of their storm-ruined homes?
Their shadows soar and switch on the blonde sea-cliff
as the sun doubles their dance.
What joke of evolution induced birds to burrow,
like rabbits, in sand — storm petrels, shear-waters,
orange-booted puffins, sand martins —
birds who spend so long on the wing, on the sea
they can't prove title to rock, bush or tree?

II

When I was very small, there was a big family
who tumbled into school, always late, with unkempt,
pudding-bowl haircuts, always full of excuses
about missed days, undone homework and sore throats.
We knew that, most years, they arrived from Glasgow
to squat in a broken-down gatehouse. And one year
they did not come back, nor the next, nor ever.
And where are they now? They were just children like us.
Do they have grandchildren? Were they loved?
Did they know justice in the end?
Does even one of them own a safe, snug nest?

AILSA CRAIG
for Sarah Gatley

Carraig Alasdair,
Paddy's milestone,
Ealasaid a' Chuain.
wind-skelped isle,
high, brooding ships' marker,
foam-broken parish of sea birds,
stubborn mountain core,
stepping-stone between countries,
roost for mad Sweeney,
eyrie for goats,
backdrop for golfers,

upturned pudding-bowl
of a granite,
so fine-grained
its quarried, polished
stones are sent scudding
across frozen lakes for sport.

And, as if to prove
that everything,
in the long storm of time,
can become its opposite

a cool knuckle of granite
buff-coloured and lapis-blue —
exotic as rhododendron
in a northern forest —
rumbled down the Irish sea
by long-gone glaciers
and today's tides,
gleams, this morning,
by my shoe,
betraying nothing
of a dizzy history,
a hell-hot source.

NEIGHBOUR
i.m. Harry Alcorn

The war had made a tailor of him. When he came home
he served his time with Davey Stuart. Forty years later
we would push through a hole in the hedge
and climb up onto the bench with him to hunt
for big spools among scraps of thorn-proof suiting.
My sister was there one day when his new leg arrived.

We'd share the brass-studded leather settee
with his disabled wife, waiting impatiently
for the test card to go and for *Blue Peter*
to light up on a small, brown, Bush TV,
which was everlastingly tuned to BBC,
and one day we saw him gently comb her hair.

When we were leaving, he'd reach up to a high press
and come back with a wrapped sweet each.
Working in Scotland, he'd 'listed, with a friend,
at seventeen, after another white-feather taunt.
For a year, he served at the front.
Every November, he used to lay the wreath.

When we were older and questioned him
he didn't say much, told my brother of a sergeant
who was good to him in the training camp
in Rossie, where they also taught reading.
As a boy in Horn Head, school was miles away
down a steep road and he was useful on the farm.

He mentioned 'revally' and foraging, chasing
after chickens in France; places called 'Arras' and 'Wipers';
'You were up and down them trenches that much
you wouldn't know where you were.' He'd met
Italian troops, 'Tidy wee men in tidy wee uniforms'.
Now, as he took the measure of small farmers,

brought them back for unhurried fittings,
the stories of the townlands flowed in to him
as he pinned and chalked. Though discreet,
he had mastered the art of seamless speech —
he stood, talking, in the doorway on his stick
as customers reluctantly attempted retreat.

At eighty-six he fell and broke a collar bone
and was happy, at first, in the veterans' hospital
in Dublin — a party, 'a wee half'un',
old army songs. But two months later
they'd stopped strapping on his wooden leg
and he lay in the iron bed, his flow

of slow, droll talk dried up like a summer burn
because neither nurse nor orderly knew how to turn it on.
I held his bruised-looking, blue-veined hand,
and at last heard him murmur, 'I want to hear the water'.
Next day, two neighbours and my father
drove four hundred miles to bring him home.

My mother claimed it was the Lourdes water
they gave him when he passed out near Omagh
that brought him the last bit. Whatever about that papish sip,
he rallied and lived ten years more, near the shore.
We never heard what he suffered or did, as empires poured
young men's lives, like grains of sand, into Flanders mud.
He remembered that 'bawn' was the French for *good*.

DONEGAL TARANTELLA
for Ronan Galvin

Tunes wash up, ocean-polished pebbles,
in the kitchens of south Donegal —
mazurkas, germans, highlands, hornpipes, jigs, reels,
all gone native since they were washed in
by waves of returning emigrants,
Napoleonic garrisons,
travelling pipers or fiddling tinsmiths.

And in one fiddling family
a tarantella was passed down
from a time before the famine,
before there was a fiddle in any house,
when shelter was afforded to a sailor,
rescued from the wreck of the *Grassen* —
out of Bergen, bound for Naples -
who, one night at a house dance,
joined in the lilting,
with a tune from his native Italy,
to please a girl or
to keep the dancers going
on a floor of beaten clay,
a new tune, a gift,
a ringing coin,
tossed into the trove
of northern music.

THE BOY WHO SWAPPED A BOG FOR A GRAMOPHONE
for Eddie O'Gara

The boy, a musician already at fourteen,
walked four miles with his brother
along the Glen Road
to the fair in Carrick.

When they had seen enough
of sheep and huckster stalls,
they noticed a gramophone
and gathered up courage
to ask the shopkeeper
to play a record.

They hung about so long,
listening and wondering
that the shopkeeper, who knew
the mountainy townland
they came from — Mín na bhFachrán,
named for healing bogbine,
known for music —
proposed a barter,
the gramophone for turf-cutting rights.

The boys walked home,
taking turns to carry the gramophone
and three records.
We don't know how many cartloads of turf
the shopkeeper took out of the bog
or for how many summers
or what the boys' father,

a fiddler in a valley of fiddlers, said
or who got the better part of the bargain,
only that they had dry turf in Carrick that winter
and that a new music was played
all down the valley.

GLENCOLMCILLE SOUNDTRACK

All day long, as I climbed,
in sunshine, up to the holy well,
then on to the Napoleonic watchtower,
and halted behind it, on a headland
tramped brown by sheep,
to watch the sea carve slow blue paths
through cliffs and skerries,
May's soundtrack played on and on —
bee-hum, the high *meheh* of hill-lambs,
the lifted songs of larks in warm grass
and later, near the court tomb in the valley,
the cuckoo's shameless call.

How did we forget it,
mislay or roll it up?
— this tapestry of sound
which pleasured us
by spilling hawthorn hedges
in whin-scented summer,
as pools of yellow iris
were conjured out of wet fields
and late bluebells, vetch and fern
recaptured the ditches.

'SONGS LAST THE LONGEST...'
for Susan Hiller

my mother, who could not sing, told me.
As a young woman, she helped garner
the last grains of Tyrone Irish.
A teetotaller, her job
was to carry the whiskey bottle
which uncorked memory —
'the old people remembered scraps of songs
when they remembered nothing else.'

And today I heard a recorded lullaby
sung by a woman long dead,
in Kulkhassi, a language also dead.

No one understands the words
or knows what the singer might have sung
to an infant who may be a grandparent today
walking, haltingly, in the shade,
down a street in South Africa.

Did she sing about stars, or rain,
or tall grass, or blue flowers,
or small boats on a quick, brown river
or antelopes in a mountain valley
or a dark spirit who might snatch away a little child.

Whatever promises or prayers
the song's words held
in that forever lost language
the mystery remains
that any infant on this hurried earth
could still feel the lullaby's intent.

Through its rhythms and syllables
love pours still
like milk
through a round sieve.

WHERE IS MUSIC STORED
for Leo and Clare

in a small corner
of the human brain,
the bird's brain,
in the subtle intelligence of water?

Or is it hoarded
in the muscles and sinews
of human hands and arms,
of a human throat,
a bird's throat,
or in the stone and silver throat,
of a mountain rivulet?

A musician recalls a tune
she hasn't played for years,
discovers it like a book on a high shelf,
a fine scarf slipped down the back of a wardrobe,

Strings, keys, are fingered tentatively,
brain cells call up mathematical patterns,
a tune starts to flow,
to find form, clear and quick,
in the vibrating air —
cadences which permit us to share
our unworded joy, yearning, despair.

THE RECORDS

have come down from the attic
to fill a low shelf.
Serious investments,
unsleeved, the needle dropped,

they were the black magic
which allowed beautiful, long-haired
America, in bell-bottomed jeans and garlands,
to stroll into our college bedsits,
to sit cross-legged and play guitar.
Simon and Garfunkel, Dylan and Joan Baez
sang through a joss-stick haze
while wax dripped from homemade candles.

We imprinted on the singer or band,
whose vibration matched our timbre,
whose songs seemed to understand,
the storm clouds in our hearts, blood, minds -
Crosby, Stills, Nash and Young, Steeleye Span,
Joni Mitchell, the bearded folk musicians,
the traditional songs and tunes
which sang through us, as though our bones knew
the music, long before a gold-tipped bow
drew it out of strings and wood, or it flowed
from the chanter, the wrist-played drones.

On the scuffed, square record sleeves
the musicians remain handsome and young;
I am not sixteen or twenty-one
and don't want to return
to the inner hurricanes
of those tossed, bewildered years.
But our records gave us rough-drawn charts
of oceans of yearning, bliss and fear,
so, warped and scratched LPs,
play on, play on, play us on.

A SENTIMENTAL EDUCATION

On the brown wireless with the dented mesh
Bing Crosby sang
Oh, my name is McNamara,
I'm the leader of the band.
I marched up and down the brown-tiled kitchen,
as my mother washed dishes,
soaped and starched shirt collars
ironed, and we both sang tunelessly along.

Andy Stewart sang,
There was a soldier, a Scottish soldier...
Even at three or four, I felt that soldier's homesickness -
Because those green hills are no' Highland hills
They're no' island hills, they no' my land hills...
Felt, maybe, her homesickness, too,
for her green hills of Tyrone.

Elvis sang,
Can't you see that I love you?
Please don't break my heart in two.
I sang in puzzlement and she tried to explain,
Wooden heart, heart break
but how does a small child know metaphor?

Odetta sang
I know where I'm going
and I know who's going with me.
And I sang it endlessly, ecstatically,
before we went, just her and me
on the bus and train to visit her old home.

There was even a song which we sang
when she washed our hair on Saturday night
with Fairy soap and our eyes stung —
Hang down your head Tom Dooley
hang down your head and cry.
And then she towelled my hair hurriedly
combed and parted it,
and tried to encourage a quiff.

THE COUNTERMANDING ORDER, 1916

And my young grandmother, what of her?
Was she, too, dejected?
No documentary evidence exists.
My mother, too young, at seven months,
to remember, herself, used tell us,
'She heard the horse and trap in the yard again
and could not believe her ears.'

What was my grandmother doing?
Did she clear away a half-eaten Easter dinner
talking, distractedly, to her two little boys,
as she scraped jelly from a glass bowl?
Did she mix feed for hens or pigs,
or wonder about bringing cattle in for milking?
Did she pray, or take out her handwork?
Was she putting the baby down for her rest?

Only hours earlier, in the swept farmyard,
she had said goodbye to her husband of six years,
her exiled lover of seven more,
whose letters had been carried in steamships
across Caribbean and Atlantic tides.

On this Sunday morning, had they embraced
as he headed for the muster at Dungannon?
— as he enjoined her to bring up the children
as 'good Catholics and good Irishmen and Irishwomen'.
(My mother, in old age, was to remark, with a raised eyebrow,
'Wasn't it a bit cool of him, all the same?')

Now, as the trap clattered in through the gate
and the horse, Rebel, halted in his familiar place,
did my young grandmother wipe her hands on her apron,
did she rush to the door?

Although the Rising had been called off,
although the great cause seemed lost again,
did her heart not rejoice?

OCTOBER 1945

It was two months later
two months after a small sun
opened its belly over the city
and pressed Hiroshima into the ground.

After two months of trudging
and turning rubble she found it
under a melted bottle — her daughter's
scorched wooden sandal,
There was no mistaking the straps
she had made from her old kimono.

HARD LESSONS

Five hundred Hiroshima schoolgirls
and their teachers
had been pulling down
wooden houses,
removing clay tiles.
to create a fire-break
for fear of bombing raids.

The sculptor gives us three of them,
three thirteen-year-olds
two with plaits, one with bobbed hair,
holding a box marked with $E=mc^2$.

Beside the loveliest building in the world,
a white flower on a silk-blue sky,
between the ribbed arches of the women's pavilion,
bees have swarmed.

Their hive is a brown blob
in the rose-coloured roof.
The bees hardly notice the awed, exhausted crowds
draped in multi-coloured silk, cotton and nylon
who press far below them each day.
They may not even notice
the white palace built for a dead wife.

By the long narrow ponds
they plunder the flowers —
pink and blue forget-me-nots;
they dodge the white, long-limbed egrets
who high-step among the blossoms.
The bees neither know nor care
that the beloved queen, the favoured wife,
died near a battlefield,
having birthed her fourteenth child,
or that, to build the floating dome,
white marble slabs were balanced
on the backs of elephants and hauled,
for three and a quarter miles,
up a spiral wooden ramp
which was dismantled in a night.

The bees have their own work to do.
They have a hive to build,
a queen to serve,
larvae to feed,
honey to make.

SAINT PATRICK'S WELL, ORVIETO
(*Pozzo di San Patrizio, Orvieto*)
for Eiléan and Macdara

When Pope Clement VII took refuge
in the high, walled city
while Rome was being sacked,
by the Holy Roman Emperor,

he feared a siege,
so had the master architect,
Antonio da Sangallo the Younger,
cut a well fifty metres

down through bedrock,
a well much deeper even, and wider
than the Etruscan well of Perugia,
almost as deep

as Saladin's well at Cairo.
Seventy internal windows
lit its two graceful staircases
which intertwined in a double helix,

so one mule could descend
the broad steps
while another toiled up
with barrels of water,

a well so deep
it almost touched Purgatory.

THE COIMBRA LIBRARIANS

In the Biblioteca Joanina,
a gilt, rococo palace for leather-bound books —
the most beautiful and precious volumes
are laid open in display cases.
Each evening, before turning out the lights,
crossing the inlaid, marble floor
and softly closing, then locking,
a small door cut out of the great door,
the librarian drapes the cases

in sheets of hide, to protect them
against dirt dropped
by the library's night guardians —

a colony of small bats
who flit between soaring oak bookcases,
who skim
between geography
and astronomy,
who zig-zag,
blindly,
between science,
history,
and the lives of saints,
who dart past
the volumes
of the Procedural Records
of the Inquisition,
all the dark night,
swooping
on bookworms.

SPOONS
for Marie Foley

Sometimes we write out of darkness,
sometimes out of cool morning light,
sometimes the bird-feeder is empty,
sometimes there are five goldfinches.

Who carved the first spoon?
I don't mean a seashell
or a scoop of wood.
I mean a long-handled bone spoon
which fitted into a baby's mouth
like these in the Valencia museum,
spoons six thousand years old,
discovered in the Cova de l'Or.

When did we learn to give?
First it was kisses, then milk,
then someone invented the spoon.

CORRIB
for Eva Bourke

This river drew me to live here —
its dragon-energy after a storm
as black water from the lake
leapt in standing waves at night
between high limestone walls
or surged, light-lanced in the morning —
a tumult of white under bridges.

Its foam-falling weirs are pitched
at the angle of desire;
its canals flow alongside,
then curve off,
towards some lost or broken mill-race.

I should not love it.
I have seen search boats
and firemen clustered at the last lock
and fresh bouquets sellotaped
to quayside railings
with cellophane-wrapped tributes
'to the best brother in the world...'

Since I came here
this river has seduced
so many despairing
young women and men,
who were blind as Cupid
to their own beauty,
to the loves which failed to hold them.

Yet, on a June day,
the high-shouldered heron
guards the Fishery Tower;
mullet hang thickly under the last bridge
the lit estuary brims
with swans and cormorants;
the seal swims strongly in;
the Arctic tern punctures the tide
and the river opens out to the Atlantic
like possibility itself, or a very old song.

NO PULSE

And my old home has been dismantled —
books and CDs have been pruned and boxed,
never-used soup plates and sherry glasses
returned to the charity shop,
half the furniture passed on
to friends or young relatives
and pictures shrouded in bubble-wrap.

Pink cabbage roses,
which rooted long before I did,
three decades ago,

rub against
the kitchen window,
like an old cat.

In the white-painted yard
bins are crammed to the brim;

the emptied house gleams —
a freshly washed glass —

and I drift above it in mild surprise —
a crab, who has hauled herself out
of an old carapace,
who strains to hear
departed music.

AT DOG'S BAY

This winter's storms have chewed off
half a row of dunes,
have revealed a line of midden —
a charcoal stroke across a page of clean time
burnt winkles, burnt bones, burnt wood —
hearths smoored forever by the tail-swish
of some pre-historic hurricane.

And above the midden line,
in the fresh sand-cliff,
is a crooked line of burrows —
a new city,
a twittering, cliffside pueblo,
a lively Petra,
where sand martins,
rested after their Sahara crossing,
are swallowed up and shot out
to brush the sky
with quick calligraphy,
jubilant diagonals.

IN DERRYCLARE WOODS

Sleeved in green velvet
and violets, an oak limb
thrown over the stream.

THE RING-FORTS

The scalpel-cut of the new motorway
brings them closer to our speeding minds,
so full of codes, contacts and pin numbers.

How discreet these earth rings are,
how quiet, with their sloped green banks
their muddy, cattle-trod entries,
their enclosures of briars and nettles
and, often, their cool souterrains,
their groves of trees,
their Norman keeps.

The April fields hold so many of them
as though some old god had gone crazy
with a round stamp or a giant pastry-cutter.

Apart from a mention in the annals,
a cadence of a song, a shred of a story,
we don't know much of what went on
in this or that *cathair, dún* or *lios,*
only that they are all done with war
and trouble, with love and music.
How completely erased
are the ordinary, busy lives lived
within these green circles.

Once, through a haze of illness,
I was unaccountably gladdened
driving past a snapping line of white washing
strung right across a ring-fort,
line ends lashed to two sycamores.

DEFENCE SYSTEM

Those round, squat, granite towers
were built around the coast
at immense cost
to keep Napoleon out.

He never came, and not one shot
was fired from them
at a French ship, until lately
and then, only as a salute.

Their fame derives mainly now
from the jocose account,
by a young writer,
of his friend's morning shave.

FROM THE PLANE

There is a nest of gold in the cloud
and, far below, under the Atlantic,
lie the unquiet volcanoes
as the earth rips itself open
very slowly, to stretch the ocean.

Below us flows an endless white cloudfield
with occasional holes like tiny lavender lakes
like the brown, blue and silver bog lakes
in the half-drowned edges
of Connemara and Labrador
which have almost forgotten
the volcanoes that blew them apart.

FROM ABOVE THE ENGLISH CHANNEL
for Rachel Brown

Every cloud, even the smallest tuft,
drags its own shadow behind it,
on the skin of a silver-blue sea.

Foam-followed ships are white tadpoles.
They have forsaken, and seek out,
the primal embrace of harbours.

Families of nomads walked across here
before a great inundation,
which parted land masses.

Who witnessed its beginning,
as weather grew warmer,
and growth came earlier,

as tides rose a little higher,
and land at the tide's edge
vanished for the first time?

Vincent, you would have loved it,
as Don McClean's song poured out
of the bottom left-hand corner of the reading room
of the Irish National Library,
loudly enough for all twenty-three readers,
drowsy browsers, graduate students,
academics on sabbatical,
to lift and turn startled heads —
sea-birds grazing a salt-marsh.

He sang for a whole yellow minute, maybe two,
while readers continued to shift and turn around
not quite upset that their silence had been stolen.

From her curved counter a librarian scanned the desks
and a brown-jacketed, middle-aged man tiptoed
from the catalogue section and gently
closed the lid of a Mac Air, and a long, slow
sigh came from all forty-four cherubs
who had been swinging their plump garlands
high on the green library wall since your time

and I was blown back to a bedsit on South Circular Road
where, forty years ago, I blu-tacked the poster
of your blue and yellow field of stars
at the head of my single bed, not finding it strange
that the stars should swirl like small suns in the pit of night,
not knowing it was painted a year before
you took your own aching, luminous life,

and you, not knowing, as you fought your darkness
and frenziedly harvested the light of stars and sickle moon,
how it would be poured into a song,
how your brush would flood a library across the sea,
a century later, with golden, starry light.

RELATIVITY — THE IVEAGH GARDENS FORTY-FIVE YEARS LATER

I used to sit here in May sunshine,
a trespasser, at sixteen, studying for an exam,
trying to concentrate on a book
about the origins of the Second World War.

The university garden was a neglected demesne
of tumbled statues in the undergrowth
and silent fountains. The war had ended
long ago, well before I was born.

The holly trees must have been overgrown then.
There must have been wrens in the bushes, as today
but I do not remember them.
My life was in the future tense, after the exam.

I sat on a bench somewhere here
near this statue of Diana the Huntress
who has lost her head, her hands, her bow
and her arrows, all but for one feather.

The span of years arrowing back to that May
is far greater than from then to the end
of the Second World War
but it feels like no time at all.

POST BOX IN WALL AT ROSBRIN

Its mouth overflows with blossoms and starry leaves:
it has had enough of good news and bad,
of memoriam cards, boxes of wedding cake,
birthday cards, love letters, air-letters,
postal orders, ten-shilling notes, letters
to the Co. Council, the Solicitor, the Editor.

A shower of pink, ivy-leafed toadflax has colonised it,
hiding the symbol of the queen or king,
Free State or Republican government,
who authorised its installation here,
in a freshly plastered wall,
now blurred with yellow lichen,
a stone's throw from where the road
wraps itself around a ring-fort.

There is no method of calculating
what weight of heartbreak and passion,
of joy and gossip, it has swallowed
during the decades in which
its small iron torso held in trust
the myriad privacies of a town land.

Long retired, its traffic passed on
to laptops which post news instantly,
casually, some alchemy has caused
all the near-archaic endearments
to rise to the top, to brim from its mouth
in a cascade of tiny, pink flowers —

Dear Sir, Dear Minnie,
My Dear Patrick,
A Stóirín, Dearest John,
My Darling, Dear Daddy,
faithfully, sincerely, fondly,
affectionately, yours,
ever, ever yours.

ANOTHER GREAT MAN DOWN
Zane Grey in the Davenport Hotel, Spokane, Washington

Wyoming, The Shepherd of Guadeloupe, Under the Tonto Rim,
my big brothers' outgrown cowboy books.
I wore out the romantic sections, fell in love
with all those courageous rough diamonds,
riding up atop the Mesa, or down deep canyons,
rounding up ornery steers for honest ranchers,
cooking beans and sourdough pancakes out on the range,
arriving home to their bunkhouses in need of shut-eye,
yet ever ready to leap up to quench fires in flaming barns,
or rescue hosses or steers from doggone rustlers.
Respectful, even shy with women,
they always got the purty gal in the end.

As swirling desert dust, tumbleweed and jingling spurs
cancelled out slanting rain, gaberdine coats and October Devotions,
I never expected, fifty years later, to cross paths with Zane Grey.
He was here too, in the 1920s grandeur of the Davenport.
After a luncheon with the Chamber of Commerce
he wrote about the honest ranchers who met here
to craft a plan to break a strike of seasonal workers,
of Wobblies, riff-raff, trouble-makers, itinerant harvest workers,
arriving from the east on trains, among them maybe even
some of my own distant kin, hoping for work,
a living wage, on the round-hilled wheat fields of Washington.
And I took you for one of the good guys, Zane Grey!

AT DUSK

Last night, the fox padded along
our red-brick street
under yellow fan-lights;

last week an otter,
curved and sleek as a cat,
slipped across the pier in the half-light
and went down into the sea,
leaving quick prints on stone steps;

last month we saw a wild boar
and her three young
cross a road before dark
and vanish into the briars.

Her path was a track of mud
straight down a field
from the mountain forest
as it had been, months earlier,
a line of hoof-marks in snow
and, earlier still,
a crease in summer grass.

The creatures of dusk,
whom we have almost dispossessed,
continue to cross our paths,
continue to bless us.

CLOWANSTOWN FISH-TRAPS, 5,000 BC
National Museum of Ireland

'I must gather my traps',
she said it so often, gathering up
handbag, headscarf, string shopping bag —
I never thought to ask what kind of traps —
mouse traps, rabbit snares, badger traps?
or did the phrase come from eel-fishers,
who wove branches into tricksy cones.

Two thousand years before blocks of stone
were hauled to build the Pyramids,
branches of birch, alder and rosewood
were cut, twisted into four long cones,
wedged or staked in a weir or narrow stream,
and one day, left ungathered.

They were hardly forgotten,
like a mobile phone or keys.
Some interruption — illness, death,
the season's push to move on,
or an enemy raid, a wrecking storm,
swept four traps into this glass case.

And, still, after St Patrick's Day,
when Arctic terns fly back
from South Africa to fall, white darts,
on sand-smelts in a Connemara lagoon,
a man will walk by a small stream
and wedge or stake conical fish traps.

GOLD
for Fionnuala and Reva-Ann

A century ago today
my grandmother held on
to the rods of an iron bedstead
as she pushed her first daughter
out into autumn light
which shafted
between the drawn curtains
of a northern farmhouse window.

'Maureen's hair', she said,
'is the colour of a new sovereign.'

9/9/2015

IN MEMORIAM
Rose Cannon 1920 — 2016

Yesterday I saw my little, blue-eyed aunt,
still lovely after almost a century,
go, so quietly, so willingly, into the good night,
or the good light, she might already
have been aboard a reed boat,
afloat on a morning river.

'Fill up the room', she had told her friend,
and in that sun-filled room,
with her big, mechanised chair,
her stuffed bookcase, and little else,
her friends came and went all day.
They held her hands, stroked her forehead,
chatted softly, and, at the end,
said prayers she had learned
as a small girl in Donegal.

When I put my hand on her arm
I felt only bone.
Over the last months
she had become a reed herself
and spoke the word 'love' more often,
with less embarrassment,
than anyone I have known.

THE TWELVE BENS...
 for Lynn

yesterday morning, striding
in their shawls of rain and, later,
sun-blasted, and today
dappled under running clouds.

I start to understand why we love them,
not just their hard grey,
white and blue beauty
but also their companionability

as they pose together
in a semicircle behind the lake,
a group of friends,
arms around each others' shoulders,

as we did yesterday
smiling at the camera,
remembering our late, great friend
who loved the Glencoaghan Horseshoe;

loved to name the mountains,
Derryclare, Ben Lettery, Bengowar;
who gathered us together yesterday
between mountains and estuary,

in a blue and white house
with seven welcoming doors.

THE SONG OF THE BOOKS (AMHRÁN NA LEABHAR)
for Seamus and Bronagh

It's the plummeting second note
that knells his despair
two centuries later —
his clothes and all
his leather-bound books
drifted down among the kelp
off Derrynane —
his own poems,
his rare manuscripts in Irish,
blurring underwater,
turning to pulp
among crabs and mackerel
and the poet-schoolmaster,
who had travelled overland,
getting word
by the shore in Port McGee,
and making a song
out of utter loss.

It was not the library of Alexandria
whose shelved scrolls stored
the known world's wisdom
and claimed to cure souls,
or the library of Nineveh
or of Babylon,
where kings had imprinted
their triumphs on wet clay,

yet the bell-voiced singers
and the uilleann pipers tell it
as though the wooden sailing boat
with its small, treasured library,
identity papers of the dispossessed,
had hit that sea-hid rock,
had gone down
only yesterday.

CLIMB

A worn quartzite cone,
the mountain sails on
in and out of mist.
Below, a hundred islands come and go —
doors of perception blow open, blow closed.

VII
NEW POEMS

A SONG AT IMBOLC

Now at spring's wakening, short days are lengthening
and after St. Bridget's Day, I'll raise my sail.
Antoine Ó Raifteirí

A blind man, on a stone bridge in Galway
or the road to Loughrea, felt the suns's rays
in his bones again and praised the sycamore and oak,
crops still drowsy in the seed, wheat, flax and oats.
His song rising, he praised Achill's eagle, Erne's hawk
and in beloved Mayo, young lambs, kids, foals,
and little babies turning towards birth.

Blind Raftery invoked Bridget, Ceres of the North,
born into slavery at Faughert, near Dundalk
to an Irish chieftain and a foreign slave.
Why, of all small girls in so distant a century born
is she honoured, still, in place-names, constant wells,
new rushes plaited to protect hearth, home and herd?

Bridget, goddess, druidess of oak, or saint — a girl
who gifted her father's sword to a beggar for bread,
we, who have wounded the engendering seas and earth,
beg you to teach us again, before it grows too late,
your neglected, painstaking arts of nurture and of care.

DELETE CONTACT CARD

It's happening more often now —
going through my contacts list
I find the name of an old friend,
a decade or more older than me,
with whom I spent sunlit afternoons,

laughing and talking about life and poetry
and I don't delete the card —
as though a computer list could
hold a soul for a month, a year, or more
in some limbo or bardo.

Rain falls on the red bushes
The talkative postman
still delivers books and letters,
and, with a small thump,
a goldfinch lands on the window feeder.

Life does go on without the dead
and, no matter how much we wish it,
we won't ever know for certain
whether or not the dead watch over us
until our own cards await deletion.

What we do know now, better
than we used to, is the worth
of that honeycomb of hours
spent laughing and talking —
the sunwashed, unwasted hours
of human contact.

PASCAL

The eternal silence of these infinite spaces terrifies me.
Blaise Pascal

You understood so much as you stood in awe
of our long-armed swirl of stars
burning their huge hearts out—

yet you didn't know that there were other,
far more distant, worlds of light,
that our spinning, sea-blue earth,
our sun and sister planets,
are smaller than salt grains
in the dark, rushing theatre of space.

You didn't know that we,
our eyebrows, livers, ankles, thumbs,
are made of old stars blown to dust
then, somehow, sprung to life,
that our distant, minute, unthinking ancestors
might have bubbled up through an ocean floor
or hurtled in on the frozen fragment of a star.

You, who believed that the supreme function
of reason is to show us
that some things are beyond reason,
did you, in your faith and wondering,
still strive to fix and hold steady a platform,
high above us and our sun, to accommodate,
in golden rows, the mystery of cherubim,
seraphim, the righteous dead,
God's saints, the trinity enthroned?

We, who grew up with reason enthroned,
who have learned how to weigh a star
and measure a billion years of light,
who have blurred the plush black
of your silver-studded night
with our small, insistent lamps,

we wonder, still, what lies
beyond the rim of a universe
which may have no edge at all
in either space or time, which may fold
back upon itself in deepest mystery

as, above and around us,
planets spin out their very long
or their very short days, as red giants,
white dwarves and supernovae grow,
implode, burn out, collide
yet continue to come to birth.

TAKING THE BRUNT OF IT

I pick them up in the sunny park every morning,
to bring home and put in a glass jug.
They are mostly short-stemmed,
bent and broken by April gusts.
I did not know there were so many different kinds —
orange fringed suns, yellow trumpets,
dainty white dancers, saffron flouncers.

The brave narcissi, up
and out on strong green stems,
lifting their heads to the sun,
taking the brunt of spring storms —
a few young ones snap at the root
but, mostly, it's the older ones,
with weakened stems,
which bend and break.

And in this storm
which rips across the world,
which has grounded air fleets,
and emptied teeming streets,
it's the older ones,
who sit, heads nodding,
in tall-backed chairs,
who try to smile into the phone,
so many different beloved ones,
who take the brunt of it.

09/04/20

LIGHT IS WHAT DAYS ARE MADE OF —

it pulls the daffodil up out of dark earth,
prompts the eagle and the stub-tailed wren to nest
and draws the humpback whale north with its song.

Stones, warm on the morning sea-shore, know it.
Our sun is so much older than them —
such tempests of grief it has scanned
yet light, like love, eternally draws us on.

P. 10, 'TAOM'

Taom: Gaelic: 'an overflowing', usually in the context of a great wave of emotion.

P. 41, CRANNÓG

Crannóg: Gaelic, 'Lake dwelling,' (Iron age and early Christian period.)

P. 89, RÚN

Rún: Gaelic, 'Secret'

P. 97, WHIN

Sliotar: Gaelic, ball used in the game of hurling.

P. 109, BANNY

Beannaigh: Gaelic, to bless, to greet.

P. 141, LADY GREGORY AT CILL GHOBNAIT

Cill Ghrá an Domhain: Church of the Love of the World, old name for Cill Ghobnait.

P. 213, MOLAISE

A thirteenth-century wooden statue of the sixth-century Irish saint Molaise was, until the 1950s, kept in a building known as St Molaise's House, in the monastic settlement on the island of Inishmurry off the Sligo coast. The statue was traditionally removed from the house and venerated on the saint's feast day. In the eighteenth century an attempt was made by Loftus Jones of Ballisodare to burn it as an idol. It is currently housed in the Collins Barracks section of the Irish National Museum.

P.274, THE COUNTERMANDING ORDER
The Countermanding Order was an order issued by Eoin
MacNeill, Commander-in-Chief of the Irish Volunteers,
and published in the *Sunday Independent*, Dublin, on Easter
Sunday 1916. Its aim was to prevent the countrywide
uprising planned by a secret military committee drawn
from the Irish Volunteers and Irish Citizen Army, including
Patrick Pearse, Thomas Clarke, Thomas McDonagh and
James Connolly.

P.288, THE RINGFORTS
cathair, dún, lios, Gaelic terms for ring-forts.

P. 295, POSTBOX IN WALL AT ROSBRIN
a stóirín, Gaelic, 'my little treasure'.

P.303, THE SONG OF THE BOOKS
Amhrán na Leabhar was written by the poet-schoolmaster,
Tomás Rua O Súilleabháin (1785–1848). He had been
transferred from Derrynane, near the southern tip of the
Iveragh Peninsula in Co. Kerry, to Portmagee, twenty-five
miles further north. The boat on which his precious books
and his other belongings were being transported sank shortly
after leaving Derrynane. It is possible that the very beautiful
melody predated the song and may have been a harping air.

P.309, 'A SONG AT IMBOLC'
Commissioned by Galway, 2020, European City of Culture.

P. 314, 'LIGHT IS WHAT DAYS ARE MADE OF'
Commissioned by RTÉ as part of its 'Shine Your Light'
project, Easter, 2020.

INDEX OF TITLES